# *Praise for* **BARBACOA**

"*Barbacoa* is a must-have book to include in your arsenal of cookbooks. You will learn to create Tex-Mex barbecue, from smoked meats to sauces and salsas to sides and desserts, that your friends and families can experience and enjoy. And *Barbacoa* is much more than just a cookbook. It is a story told through Brandon Hurtado's eyes that pays homage to the traditions and flavors that he and all Tejanos grew up with, myself included. Bring the family together, light the pit, and start making memories!"

　　—From the Foreword by Ernest Servantes, Burnt Bean Co. BBQ, Seguin, Texas

"In *Barbacoa*, Brandon Hurtado brings to life a cooking tradition that is revered and sacred in Mexican and Mexican-American cultures. Anyone who reads this book will come to appreciate, understand, and master the art of barbacoa. I am happy that this book exists—it has tons of technique guidance and loads of big-flavor recipes. Please get to know this book. You will be more than delighted with the results."

　　—Aarón Sánchez, chef, judge on television cooking shows including *MasterChef* and *Chopped*, and author of *La Comida del Barrio* and *Simple Food, Big Flavor*

"Barbecue has evolved from an innovative means of making poor cuts of meat edible to a culinary art form. Today that evolution continues as the line between pitmaster and chef blurs to the point of disappearing. Brandon Hurtado is the embodiment of that blurred line. Fusing barbecue with other cuisines and culinary styles, riffing on themes then riffing on them again, without ever forgetting what most haute cuisine chefs always seem to forget—above all, it must taste good. Very good. To rise above the crowded field of accomplished pitmaster-chefs today is an achievement worth noting. Brandon Hurtado has done it. And he's still rising."

　　—Taylor Sheridan, actor, screenwriter, director, producer, creator of *Yellowstone*

"*Barbacoa* is a vibrant and delicious celebration of Tex-Mex barbecue. Brandon Hurtado masterfully fuses the bold flavors of Tex-Mex and the rich heritage of Mexican cuisine with the modern art of BBQ. Every dish looks incredible and backs up its looks with major flavor."

　　—Jess Pryles, author of *Hardcore Carnivore* and host of Outdoor Channel's *Hardcore Carnivore*

"Let me tell you—being a Texan means two things: loving cars and loving barbecue. I've spent my whole life around fast cars and slow-cooked meats, and when it comes to BBQ, Brandon Hurtado knows how to bring the heat. *Barbacoa* is the real deal. It's packed with everything that makes BBQ the best damn food on the planet. Brandon's got the magic touch, mixing up classic Texas flavors with a killer Tex-Mex twist. Whether you're a pitmaster or just firing up the smoker in your backyard, you'll be turning out food that'll have your friends lining up for seconds. So crack open this book and GET YOU SOME OF THAT! This is the kind of BBQ that'll make you proud."

　　—Richard Rawlings, Gas Monkey Garage, Dallas; Texan, car guy, and BBQ fanatic

# BARBACOA

## *The Heart of*

## TEX-MEX BARBECUE

## BRANDON HURTADO

HARVARD COMMON PRESS

**Quarto.com**

© 2025 Quarto Publishing Group USA Inc.
Text © 2025 Hurtado Barbecue LLC

First Published in 2025 by The Harvard Common Press,
an imprint of The Quarto Group, 100 Cummings Center,
Suite 265-D, Beverly, MA 01915, USA.
T (978) 282-9590 F (978) 283-2742

The Harvard Common Press titles are also available at
discount for retail, wholesale, promotional, and bulk
purchase. For details, contact the Special Sales Manager by
email at specialsales@quarto.com or by mail at The Quarto
Group, Attn: Special Sales Manager, 100 Cummings Center,
Suite 265-D, Beverly, MA 01915, USA.

29 28 27 26 25     1 2 3 4 5

ISBN: 978-0-7603-9273-7

Digital edition published in 2025
eISBN: 978-0-7603-9274-4

Library of Congress Cataloging-in-Publication Data
is available.

Design: Kelley Galbreath
Photography: Mason Griffin, except for Shutterstock on
pages: 8, 11, 12, 26, 50, 86, 130, 164, 172, 202, and 221
Food Stylist: Stephanie Bohn Creative

Printed in China

To my incredible wife, Hannah,
our beautiful kids, Emma, Bennett,
and McKinley. I love you.

To the friends, family, and fans who have
waited in line to support us week after week,
thank you from the bottom of my heart.

To Dennis and Salmon.

*IN MEMORY OF JOHN BROTHERTON.*

# CONTENTS

# FOREWORD
## by Ernest Servantes

**BARBACOA *IS MUCH MORE THAN*** just your average cookbook. It is a story told through Brandon Hurtado's eyes. It pays homage to the traditions and flavors that he and all Tejanos grew up with, myself included.

Tex-Mex fuses together rural Mexican cooking and cowboy cuisine to create dishes that are synonymous with Texas. This is especially true of Tex-Mex barbecue, since barbecue is arguably the signature food of Texas.

The recipes in Brandon's book bring back many memories of dishes that I had growing up in south Texas. These are dishes that brought my family together to celebrate big and small moments in our lives. With this book, readers can enjoy these recipes from their own backyards and kitchens, with their own families, anywhere in the world, not just in Texas, making memories that will be cherished for a lifetime, the way that I do mine.

I met Brandon through our shared passions of barbecue and hunting. We both own restaurants, and with that comes stress. One day we got to talking and realized that we both liked to de-stress by going hunting at any opportunity that we could get. He invited me to go duck hunting with him one season, which is something that I had never done before. That weekend was not only an epic hunt, but a great opportunity to unwind and talk Tex-Mex barbecue with one of the best in the business. It was that weekend that I got to really see first-hand Brandon's passion for all things barbecue, but especially his deep-rooted connections to Tex-Mex barbecue. I have nothing but respect for Brandon Hurtado's craft, his vision, and the creativity that he brings to his food.

*Barbacoa* is a must-have book to include in your arsenal of cookbooks. You will not be disappointed. You will learn to create Tex-Mex barbecue, from smoked meats to sauces and salsas to sides and desserts, that your friends and families can experience and enjoy, and that will create memories for them to look back to later. These memories can be a source of happiness that they will be able to renew again and again, each time beginning from a simple bite of something delicious. Bring the family together, light the pit, and start making memories!

**ERNEST SERVANTES**
*Co-Owner*
*Burnt Bean Co. Barbecue*
*Seguin, Texas*

# MY BARBACOA PASSION

**CURNONSKY, KNOWN AS** the Prince of Gastronomy, once said that "In cooking, as in all the arts, simplicity is the sign of perfection." Barbecue is, perhaps, one of the only cooking methods in the modern culinary world that is overly simple yet incredibly complicated at the same time. Fire. Wood. Salt. Pepper. Smoke. It's been done that way for decades, if not centuries—by Czech and German settlers in the 1800s, who first introduced their own style of sausages and smoked meats to the Texas hill country.

But long before European immigrants made their mark on Texas barbecue, Spanish conquistadors and missionaries discovered that "barbecue" was being cooked and sold by locals in Tenochtitlan, or modern-day Mexico City. Spanish explorers found many types of barbecue being cooked across the south—from Mississippi to the Caribbean—with similar methods used by Indigenous People to cook very different proteins.

Fast-forward to the nineteenth century and barbecue looked much different across the southwest.

In Texas, ranchers would give the discarded heads from butchered cattle to their vaqueros, or Mexican ranch hands, who would then cook the whole cow heads wrapped in burlap over mesquite wood coals overnight. According to José Ralat, taco editor at *Texas Monthly*, these "barbacoyeros" cooked not just out of ingenuity, but also to survive.

Today, barbacoa is a staple of Mexican cuisine, with different cooking methods and cuts of meat varying from state to state. From goat and sheep to beef, pork, chicken, and even jackrabbit, barbacoa takes different forms in modern Mexico depending on where you throw a dart on a map. However, in Texas, beef is king and it's the same when it comes to the type of barbacoa we prefer. And when it comes to Mexican food and the type Texans prefer, we actually don't prefer authentic Mexican food at all, so we made our own version of it a couple hundred years ago.

You see, in Texas, we have three major food groups: barbecue, comfort food, and *Tex-Mex*. You can throw a rock from your front door in Dallas–Fort Worth and hit a Babe's Chicken, Hard Eight (or Bill Miller's if you're in central Texas), or a Rosa's Café, if you're lucky. And while Tex-Mex food is incredibly common—*and delicious*—many Texans and Mexican Americans grew up eating a Tex-Mex fusion of barbecue that is just now gaining popularity across the United States.

I grew up a half-Hispanic kid in South Irving, Texas, who was too white to be Mexican and too Mexican to be white. I spoke enough Spanish to order food from El Fenix, but not quite enough to hold a steady conversation with my grandmother.

Our family had no culinary background beyond the backyard. In fact, I never even worked in a restaurant before owning one.

I was introduced to brisket at around seven or eight years old, when I watched my dad tend a fire on his offset smoker, cooking what seemed like one hundred briskets for his company Christmas party. How he fit one hundred briskets on a fifty-gallon smoker is something I'm still trying to figure out.

My *real* passion for barbecue didn't begin until I was around thirty years old. I cooked in my backyard for friends and family occasionally, trying to perfect a craft I knew nothing about. I took notes, recorded videos, cooked in the rain, and tried to get better with every smoke session. My now-wife and I started small, cooking at local breweries on weekends for anyone willing to pay to try our food. We sold food under umbrellas before graduating to a food trailer we bought on Craigslist, which was an oven in itself during the Texas summer months.

At one of our first pop-up events, we served brisket and pulled pork tacos, which were things I grew up eating as delicacies. Our sides weren't the traditional potato salad and baked beans. Instead, we served smoked elote on the cob, charro beans, and Mexican rice. We didn't know what to call it at the time, but we knew it represented who we were. After a few weekends, a local newspaper wrote a review that highlighted our smoked meats and Tex-Mex sides, referring to our style of cooking as "Mexicue"—and Hurtado Barbecue was born.

Perhaps you've read cookbooks written by chefs who've prepared some of the best steaks in the world, or were trained classically by French chefs in Lyon before starting their own restaurants in New York. That's not what this book is about and that's not who I am.

This book is the product of a passion project turned obsession from a former marketing executive who opened a restaurant having never worked in one before. It's the story of a family-owned business born during a pandemic and includes the recipes that helped the restaurant grow from a pop-up barbecue concept to an independently owned, multi-unit success.

It's a modern-day tale of the American dream.

It's about *barbacoa*.

Barbacoa is everything that we do at our restaurants each day—from smoking beef briskets in 120°F (49°C) sweltering heats to braising beef cheeks in Big Red soda for use on a tostada the next morning. Barbacoa was, at one point in time, a lifeline for our company when we couldn't find briskets to cook during the pandemic. It led to our first write-up in *Texas Monthly* magazine and was featured when we made the Top 50 list of barbecue restaurants in the state of Texas.

So, I hope to share with you my passion for barbacoa, as I believe there are no secrets in barbecue—only the pursuit of simplicity.

# THE
# RECIPES

# RUBS AND SAUCES

HURTADO BEEF BLEND 28 / HURTADO PORK BLEND 29 / HURTADO POULTRY BLEND 30 / MY FAJITA SEASONING 31 MY SWEET SAUCE 33 / AZTEC GOLD MUSTARD SAUCE 34 / PEACH HABANERO BARBECUE SAUCE 36 / ORIGINAL RIB GLAZE 37 / ANCHO MUSTARD VINAIGRETTE 40 / SMOKED SALSA VERDE 43 / SMOKY SALSA ROJA 44 CILANTRO LIME CREMA 47

## MY RUBS AND SAUCES were

always meant to be shared through necessity. In the early days of running my food trailer, I'd make a batch of beef blend and barbecue sauce for the day, and, by the time service ended, I'd be completely out of one or both. The next day, a team member would follow the recipes to make another batch, but there would be subtle nuances and changes. That's why I began batching my rubs and sauces in bulk through a third party— to cultivate one of the most important aspects of a good barbecue restaurant—consistency.

I didn't reinvent the wheel with my rubs or sauces. I simply used what worked, and what continues to work today. My rubs aren't overly complicated or complex, but they build a great bark and serve as a bridge between the nostalgia of classic Texas barbecue and modern Tex-Mex cuisine.

# HURTADO BEEF BLEND

This beef blend is the perfect balance of Tex-Mex barbecue. Coarse black pepper and chili powder set the tone for the blend, which creates an insane bark on anything beef—especially brisket. I use this rub in my restaurants every day on beef ribs, brisket, steaks, and more. Generally speaking, it's easier to measure spices in tablespoons or cups, but it's far more accurate to weigh them in grams to ensure your blends are correct. I'd highly suggest investing in a small kitchen scale for all your rubs and sauces.

50 grams (1.6 ounces) restaurant-style ground black pepper

45 grams (1.4 ounces) coarse black pepper

45 grams (1.4 ounces) kosher salt

25 grams (scant 1 ounce) light chili powder

25 grams (scant 1 ounce) light brown sugar

25 grams (scant ¾ ounce) seasoned salt

12 grams (scant ½ ounce) granulated garlic

1. Place all the ingredients in a shaker bottle, cover, and shake until combined well.

2. This will keep for roughly 12 months at room temperature once opened, and 2 to 3 years unopened.

# HURTADO PORK BLEND

My pork rub is just a sweeter version of my Hurtado Beef Blend (page 28). I felt like I needed something milder for pork, with a sweet finish that isn't overpowering. It still has much of the same flavor profile of the beef rub but includes granulated sugar and honey powder to help create a sweet and savory balance on ribs, pork shoulders, chops, and even seafood.

40 grams (1.4 ounces) restaurant-style ground black pepper

35 grams (1¼ ounces) light brown sugar

30 grams (1 ounce) honey powder

30 grams (1 ounce) granulated sugar

25 grams (scant 1 ounce) granulated garlic

25 grams (scant 1 ounce) light chili powder

20 grams (scant ¾ ounce) kosher salt

20 grams (scant ¾ ounce) smoked paprika

15 grams (½ ounce) seasoned salt

10 grams (⅓ ounce) onion powder

1. Place all the ingredients in a shaker bottle, cover, and shake until combined well.

2. This will keep for roughly 12 months at room temperature once opened, and 2 to 3 years unopened.

# HURTADO POULTRY BLEND

When I first started making rubs, I had two recipes: beef and pork. I used the beef blend (see page 28) on, well, beef—and the pork blend on everything else. As the company grew from a pop-up project to a multi-unit success, I realized I needed more variety in the protein flavor profiles that better complemented the meats. So, I sat down with my team and tested new rub recipes over the course of a week, landing on this blend for turkey, quail, and chicken. It has the same salt and pepper combination that lets you know we're in Texas, but with a citrusy finish of coriander notes that highlight poultry, and even vegetables. If you're feeling adventurous, this rub makes a great base for a jerk rub and even works well on pork ribs.

50 grams (1.4 ounces) restaurant-style ground black pepper

40 grams (1¼ ounces) kosher salt

30 grams (1 ounce) honey powder

35 grams (scant 1 ounce) granulated sugar

30 grams (scant ¾ ounce) light brown sugar

20 grams (⅓ ounce) seasoned salt

10 grams (⅓ ounce) granulated garlic

10 grams (⅓ ounce) smoked paprika

5 grams (⅙ ounce) orange juice powder

5 grams (⅙ ounce) ground coriander

5 grams (⅙ ounce) ground white pepper

1. Place all the ingredients in a shaker bottle, cover, and shake until combined well.

2. This will keep for roughly 12 months at room temperature once opened, and 2 to 3 years unopened.

# MY FAJITA SEASONING

There's nothing quite like a good fajita seasoning that can double as the base for a marinade. This rub is slightly more citrusy than your typical fajita seasoning but works well for both beef and chicken. You can find most of the oddball ingredients, like orange juice powder, on Amazon, and Tajín makes a good substitute for chile lime salt if unavailable.

40 grams (1.4 ounces) restaurant-style ground black pepper

30 grams (1 ounce) granulated garlic

30 grams (1 ounce) light brown sugar

25 grams (scant 1 ounce) kosher salt

25 grams (scant 1 ounce) seasoned salt

25 grams (scant 1 ounce) orange juice powder

20 grams (scant ¾ ounce) chile lime salt

20 grams (scant ¾ ounce) smoked paprika

10 grams (⅓ ounce) dried Mexican oregano

10 grams (⅓ ounce) cayenne pepper

10 grams (⅓ ounce) onion powder

5 grams (⅙ ounce) ground white pepper

5 grams (⅙ ounce) ground cumin

1. Place all the ingredients in a shaker bottle, cover, and shake until combined well.

2. This will keep for roughly 12 months at room temperature once opened, and 2 to 3 years unopened.

# MY SWEET SAUCE

Barbecue sauce is a strange thing, even in the barbecue world. In the Carolinas, it's a staple that *always* accompanies pork or chicken. In Memphis, St. Louis, and Kansas City, barbecue sauce varies so much in type and taste, but they all have in common the *necessity* for sauce. In Texas, we're arrogant and think our smoked meats stand on their own. But one thing I've learned from listening to customers is that they want sauce, so I give it to them. This sweet sauce is ideal for chopped beef sandwiches or to use with pulled pork. It's the perfect balance of sweet and tang, which I really like to cut through the richness of the smoked meats. And if you haven't had brisket foldover sandwich with a couple slices of homemade dill pickles and sweet sauce on Martin's bread, you haven't lived life.

---

2 cups (480 g) ketchup
1 cup (240 ml) water
½ cup (120 g) packed light brown sugar
½ cup (170 g) molasses
¼ cup (60 ml) apple cider vinegar
2 tablespoons (30 ml) Worcestershire sauce
2 tablespoons (30 g) Dijon mustard
1 teaspoon granulated garlic
1 teaspoon onion powder
1 teaspoon cayenne pepper
½ teaspoon smoked Spanish paprika
1 teaspoon kosher salt, plus more as needed
1 teaspoon restaurant-style ground black pepper

1. In a medium-size saucepan over medium-low heat, combine all the ingredients and stir well to mix. Bring to a simmer and cook for 15 to 20 minutes until the sauce thickens and darkens in color. It should have a "loose," or slightly watery, consistency.

2. Taste the sauce and add more salt as needed.

3. Transfer the sauce to Mason jars or squirt bottles and refrigerate immediately. The sauce will keep for roughly 3 to 4 weeks.

# AZTEC GOLD MUSTARD SAUCE

Spice lovers rejoice—this sauce is for you. It offers a subtle heat from cayenne and hot sauce, but is mellowed by the honey and brown sugar. What I love about this recipe is you don't have to cook it and prep time is minimal. I use this on pulled pork specifically, but it is also great on a barbecue torta or as a dipping sauce for chicken.

1 cup (176 g) yellow mustard

1 cup (240 g) Dijon mustard

1 cup (240 ml) hot sauce (such as Valentina)

½ cup (160 g) honey

¼ cup (60 ml) apple cider vinegar

¼ cup (60 ml) water

2 tablespoons (25 g) granulated sugar

2 tablespoons (28 g) light brown sugar

1 teaspoon cayenne pepper

1 teaspoon kosher salt

1 teaspoon smoked paprika

1 teaspoon restaurant-style ground black pepper

½ teaspoon onion powder

½ teaspoon granulated garlic

**1.** In a large bowl, combine all the ingredients. Whisk until the wet and dry ingredients are smooth without lumps. Transfer to Mason jars or squirt bottles. Store at room temperature (does not have to be refrigerated) for up to 6 months.

# PEACH HABANERO BARBECUE SAUCE

I was inspired to make this sauce after trying my buddy Chris Finch's barbecue sauce at a festival at AT&T Stadium in Dallas on a hot summer day. I'm not a huge habanero fan because of its lingering heat, but Finch's honey habanero sauce gives spice a whole new perspective. This sauce has canned peaches in it, but you can use fresh peaches (from Fredericksburg, if you're a diehard Texan) for a more intense fruit flavor.

3 cups (750 g) canned
   peaches with juice
2 cups (480 g) ketchup
1 cup (225 g) packed light
   brown sugar
½ cup (120 ml) apple cider
   vinegar
½ cup (120 ml) water
½ cup (170 g) molasses
1 habanero chile, seeded
1 tablespoon (15 ml)
   Worcestershire sauce
1 tablespoon (15 ml) soy sauce
1 tablespoon (15 ml) liquid
   smoke
1 tablespoon (7.5 g) dark
   chili powder
1 teaspoon Dijon mustard
1 teaspoon granulated garlic
1 teaspoon kosher salt,
   plus more as needed
1 teaspoon restaurant-style
   ground black pepper

1. In a medium-size saucepan over medium-low heat, combine all the ingredients. Stir well to mix. Bring to a simmer and cook for 15 to 20 minutes until the peaches soften. Remove from the heat and let the sauce cool for 20 to 30 minutes.

2. Using an immersion blender, purée until smooth. Taste the sauce and add more salt as needed.

3. Transfer to Mason jars or squirt bottles and refrigerate immediately. This sauce will keep for roughly 3 to 4 weeks.

# ORIGINAL RIB GLAZE

This rib glaze recipe is my original barbecue sauce while operating in a food trailer, mostly because it doesn't have to be cooked, and I was incredibly limited on cook space. Cooking the sauce, however, allows it to develop more flavor, but you can absolutely whisk all of the ingredients in a bowl and store it at room temperature for up to six months because of its acidity level.

**3 cups (720 g) ketchup**
**1 cup (240 ml) white vinegar**
**1 cup (225 g) packed light brown sugar**
**½ cup (120 ml) water**
**½ cup (170 g) molasses**
**¼ cup (60 ml) Worcestershire sauce**
**2 tablespoons (36 g) beef bouillon paste**
**2 tablespoons (15 g) dark chili powder**
**1 tablespoon (8.5 g) restaurant-style ground black pepper**
**2 teaspoons granulated garlic**
**1 teaspoon onion powder**
**1 teaspoon kosher salt**

1. In a medium-size metal bowl, mix all the ingredients with a whisk until combined.

2. Taste the sauce and add more salt as needed.

3. Transfer to Mason jars or squirt bottles and store at room temperature for up to 6 months.

# ANCHO MUSTARD VINAIGRETTE

This dressing is best when paired with pork or fish, but it's simple enough to use on greens alone. The ancho is best used whole, but you can use ancho powder if whole dried chiles aren't available in your neck of the woods. I've used this vinaigrette on double bone-in smoked pork chops with a simple arugula salad, which is a winner in our house when we want something a little lighter than traditional barbecue or Tex-Mex food.

**2 dried ancho chiles**
**½ cup (120 ml) reserved soaking water**
**¼ cup (60 ml) red wine vinegar**
**2 tablespoons (30 g) Dijon mustard**
**2 tablespoons (40 g) honey**
**1 garlic clove, minced**
**¾ cup (180 ml) extra-virgin olive oil**
**1 teaspoon kosher salt**
**1 teaspoon restaurant-style ground black pepper**

1. In a medium-size bowl, combine the ancho chiles and enough hot water to cover. Let steep and soften for 15 to 20 minutes. Once soft, remove the stems and seeds and place the chiles in a blender with ½ cup (120 ml) of the soaking water. Blend for 8 to 10 seconds.

2. Pour the ancho chile mixture through a fine-mesh sieve set over a metal bowl.

3. Add the vinegar, mustard, honey, and garlic and whisk to combine.

4. While whisking to emulsify the vinaigrette, slowly add the oil.

5. Season to taste with salt and pepper.

# SMOKED SALSA VERDE

My most memorable salsa verde is a recipe that my brother-in-law's mom made for his birthday one year. The ingredients were simple: "Jalapeños, garlic, water, and salt," she told me. I think she left out an ingredient or two, because I tried making it and there was a lot more to it than that. So, I've worked on my version of that salsa verde over the last five years. I start by smoking the veggies to add more depth of flavor and blend the salsa to make it smoother for use on tostadas, tacos, and more.

4 jalapeño peppers, stems
   removed
3 tomatillos, husks peeled
1 white onion, peeled
8 garlic cloves, peeled
½ cup (120 ml) canola oil,
   plus more for drizzling
1 bunch fresh cilantro
½ cup (120 ml) white vinegar
½ cup (120 ml) water
1 tablespoon (7.5 g) dark
   chili powder
1 tablespoon (10 g) kosher
   salt, plus more as needed
1 teaspoon restaurant-style
   ground black pepper
1 teaspoon chicken bouillon
   powder
1 teaspoon ground cumin
1 teaspoon dried Mexican
   oregano

1. Preheat a smoker to 250°F (120°C).

2. On a quarter sheet pan, combine the jalapeños, tomatillos, onion, and garlic. Drizzle with the oil and toss lightly to coat. Place the pan in the smoker and cook for 45 minutes until softened.

3. Remove the vegetables and let cool to room temperature.

4. Transfer the smoked vegetables to a blender and add the remaining ingredients. Blend on medium speed for 3 to 4 seconds until the salsa is well incorporated and the ingredients are broken down but not puréed.

5. Taste and add more salt as needed.

6. Serve immediately or refrigerate overnight for the flavors to meld even more.

**Opposite:** Smoked Salsa Verde, page 43, top, and Smoky Salsa Roja, page 44, bottom.

# SMOKY SALSA ROJA

I grew up in a household where my mom made her own salsa roja until it became a side hustle. To this day, Teresa Hurtado's "Salsa Queen" salsa has fed friends and family, and even made its way to the likes of George Strait. Her salsa is good on *anything*, but like any stubborn son, I had to do things *my way* and so I made a smoky variation— with a little more kick, too. I start with heirloom tomatoes because I believe a good salsa begins with quality ingredients. The heat level will vary depending on the size and spice of the jalapeños, but you can always add more.

2 pounds (908 g) heirloom tomatoes

2 jalapeño peppers, stems removed

1 poblano pepper, stem and seeds removed

1 medium-size white onion, peeled

4 garlic cloves, peeled

2 tablespoons (30 ml) canola oil

½ cup (8 g) chopped fresh cilantro

½ cup (120 ml) water

2 tablespoons (30 ml) white vinegar

1 tablespoon (10 g) kosher salt, plus more as needed

2 teaspoons dark chili powder

1 teaspoon restaurant-style ground black pepper

½ teaspoon ground cumin

½ teaspoon dried Mexican oregano

1. Preheat a smoker to 225°F (107°C).

2. On a half sheet pan, combine the tomatoes, jalapeños, poblano, onion, and garlic. Drizzle with the oil and toss lightly to coat. Place the pan in the smoker close to the firebox so they blister some and cook for 45 minutes to 1 hour until the vegetables are softened. Remove the vegetables and let cool to room temperature.

3. Transfer the smoked vegetables to a blender or food processor and add the remaining ingredients. Pulse for 5 to 6 seconds, or until the salsa is chunky and the ingredients are equally distributed.

4. Taste and add more salt as needed.

5. Serve immediately or refrigerate overnight so the flavors meld even more. Store in refrigerator for 3 to 4 weeks.

# SALSAS

My one rule for salsa is to start with good-quality ingredients, and you will get a better end result. There are many ways to put salsa together, so explore what works best for you.

The ones we use most in our restaurants are:

**SALSA VERDE (GREEN SAUCE):** This is traditionally a chunky, green, tomatillo-based salsa with a decent heat. Like my grandma's, it has a foundation of jalapeños, onions, and garlic, although we add tomatillos to lower the spice a bit. Salsa verde pairs well with most Mexican food. We use it on everything, such as barbacoa, street tacos, and tostadas..

**SALSA DE AGUACATE OR AVOCADO SALSA:** This is like salsa verde but with avocado blended or folded in. To keep it from oxidizing, we put the pit of the avocado in the salsa before storing it in the refrigerator. Avocado salsa is perfect for anything you want to cool down. We use it with fajita steak tacos, tacos al carbón, flank steak, and chicken—basically anything spicy.

**SALSA TAQUERIA:** We use this salsa a lot in Texas. It's what most people think of when they think of salsa. It is made with a fresh tomato base, chiles, onion, garlic, and a bit of vinegar, then cooked and blended. Salsa taqueria is served with almost anything, especially tacos.

**SALSA ROJA OR RED SALSA:** This mainstay salsa is the one you see served with chips in a Mexican restaurant. It is fresh, chunky, and rustic. You can control the heat in this salsa because it is predominantly tomatoes. We use it on chicken, fish, and fish tacos.

**PICO DE GALLO OR SALSA FRESCA:** This fresh, simple salsa is used on everything in our restaurants. The basic recipe is tomatoes, jalapeños, onion, lime, and cilantro, but you can create variations with your own additions. If possible, eat your pico de gallo the same or next day because the citrus breaks down the other ingredients as it sits.

# CILANTRO LIME CREMA

Greek yogurt isn't traditional when it comes to Tex-Mex cuisine, or barbecue for that matter, but not much of what I do is traditional. This crema is the perfect accompaniment for nachos, but can even be used on elotes with queso fresco.

1 cup (240 g) plain Greek yogurt

½ cup (120 g) mayonnaise

¼ cup (60 ml) water

2 garlic cloves, peeled

2 tablespoons (30 ml) fresh lime juice

2 teaspoons grated lime zest

1 teaspoon kosher salt

¼ cup (4 g) chopped fresh cilantro

1. In a food processor or blender, combine the yogurt, mayonnaise, water, garlic, lime juice and zest, and salt. Blend for 4 to 5 seconds, or until smooth.

2. Add the cilantro and pulse 3 to 4 times until the crema is smooth and creamy.

3. Serve immediately. Keep leftovers refrigerated, in an airtight container, for up to 4 days.

# SIDE DISHES

SMOKED ESQUITES 53 / BRISKET
CHARRO BEANS 54 / MEXICAN
RICE 56 / HATCH CHILE CHEDDAR
MASHED POTATOES 59 / HANNAH'S
GARLIC HABANERO PICKLES 61
SPICY PICKLED RED ONIONS 62
CRUNCHY KALE SLAW 65 / BACON
BRAISED CABBAGE 66 / BRISKET
ESQUITES 67 / TATER TOT CASSEROLE 70
HATCH CHILE CHEDDAR GRITS 73 / ANCHO
AIOLI BRUSSELS SPROUTS 75 / HATCH
CHILE MAC AND CHEESE 76 / AL PASTOR
WINGS 79 / SERRANO LIME SLAW 80
GARLIC CHORIZO GREEN BEANS 83

# IN BARBECUE, SIDE DISHES

are often an afterthought, with pitmasters believing that having the best brisket or pork ribs is what sets them apart. The truth is, once you've had great brisket, somewhere, you've had great brisket everywhere. About fifteen years ago, a wave of craft barbecue restaurants and food trailers started pioneering what barbecue means in Texas, beginning with the sides. People such as Wade Elkins, Evan LeRoy, Lane Milne, Ernest Servantes, and Dayne Weaver have redefined what barbecue means today—it goes far beyond the meats. Texas barbecue doesn't have the same standards today that it did twenty years ago, or even ten years ago, for that matter. Consumers expect an immersive, smoky experience. They expect great proteins, but they *want* great sides and desserts. They want to feel nostalgic when they walk into a place, but without '80s barbecue food.

They want the old *with* the new.

You may have the best brisket on the block, but if your sides are slippin', you'll be the first to hear about it (most likely on Yelp). That's why I've curated some of our most popular side dishes that helped land me on *Texas Monthly* magazine's Top 50 Barbecue Joints list in 2021. From smoked street corn to Hatch chile cheddar grits, my sides are seasonal and rotate every few months, which is part of what makes Hurtado Barbecue special.

# SMOKED ESQUITES

Let's address the elephant in the room for anyone wondering about the difference between esquites, elotes, and Mexican street corn. For one, both esquites and elotes are Mexican street corn, but esquites are served off the cob in a cup (or elote en vaso), and elotes are served on the cob with crema, queso fresco, cilantro, and chile powder. I've served all kinds, but I generally prefer esquites (off the cob) because it's easier to eat.

4 ears yellow corn, shucked

2 tablespoons (28 g) salted butter

1 teaspoon minced garlic

1 teaspoon kosher salt

½ cup (120 g) Cilantro Lime Crema (page 47)

4 tablespoons (32 g) Cotija cheese, divided

1 teaspoon chili powder

1 tablespoon (15 ml) hot sauce (such as Valentina; optional)

½ teaspoon chopped fresh cilantro

1 lime, cut into wedges

1. Preheat a smoker to 250°F (120°C).

2. Cut off both ends of the corn cobs so you have a stable base to shave the kernels. Stand the corn upright and carefully cut down each side to remove the kernels from the cobs. Place the kernels on a quarter sheet pan and place in the smoker for 25 minutes.

3. Once the kernels are smoked, in a large skillet over medium-high heat, melt the butter. Add the corn once the pan is hot. Do not move the kernels for the first minute so they get a little char, then cook them, tossing, for 1 to 2 minutes longer before turning the heat to low.

4. Add the garlic and kosher salt, and stir.

5. Add the crema and 2 tablespoons (16 g) of the Cotija cheese. Cook for 1 minute, stirring. Turn off the heat and transfer the corn to a serving bowl. Top with the remaining 2 tablespoons (16 g) Cotija and sprinkle with the chili powder.

6. Drizzle with hot sauce (if using) and garnish with cilantro and lime wedges. Serve immediately.

# BRISKET CHARRO BEANS

Charro beans are a delicacy of Mexican food that requires very little to be very good. I remember my Grandma Nico's charro beans—they were so simple and always tasted so damn good, but she rarely used more than three or four ingredients. I've tried to maintain the same simple approach to this recipe, but the real secret is soaking the beans overnight. They cook much faster the next day. You *can* use canned pinto beans (thoroughly rinsed) but don't expect the same depth of flavor in your charro beans. I usually keep a few pounds of smoked brisket vacuum-sealed in the freezer, which you can thaw, chop, and toss into the charro beans for a whole new level of savory and smoke.

---

5 pounds (2.3 kg) dried pinto beans

6 garlic cloves, peeled

4 Roma tomatoes, halved

2 jalapeño peppers

1 white onion, peeled and halved

1 cup (272 g) chipotle peppers in adobo

¼ cup (80 g) chicken base

6 dried chiles de árbol

2 bay leaves

½ cup (80 g) kosher salt

6 tablespoons (about 90 g) Hurtado Pork Blend (page 29)

2 tablespoons (14 g) ground cumin

1 cup (16 g) chopped fresh cilantro

1 pound (454 g) chopped Tex-Mex Smoked Brisket (page 89), or store-bought

1. In a large pot, combine the dried beans and 2 quarts (1.9 L) water. Let soak overnight.

2. The next morning, rinse the beans thoroughly and drain. Return the beans to the pot and cover with 1 to 2 inches (2.5 to 5 cm) fresh water. Place the pot over medium-high heat.

3. Add the garlic, tomatoes, whole jalapeños, onion halves, chipotles, chicken base, chiles de árbol, bay leaves (tie the chiles and bay leaves in a sachet, if you like), salt, pork blend, and cumin. Bring to a slow rolling boil and cook for 2½ to 3 hours over medium-high heat until the beans are soft.

4. Add the cilantro and brisket and stir to combine well.

5. Adjust the heat to maintain a simmer and let the beans cook for 30 minutes to an hour longer until the beans are tender. Remove the chiles de árbol and bay leaves before serving.

# TYPES OF
# SMOKERS

When considering a smoker, the best strategy is to consider your budget and experience level with live-fire cooking. Smokers can be thousands of dollars, but you can produce incredible products on a less expensive model—and you can always upgrade if smoking becomes your new passion.

**DRUM SMOKER:** These charcoal smokers can be set up easily by beginners and burn all day because of the large fuel basket.

**ELECTRIC SMOKER:** The benefit of these often pricy models is they require less supervision because the temperature is controlled with a dial. These smokers produce less smoke than others by using wood chips in a tray over a heating element.

**OFFSET SMOKER:** These classic wood-fueled units come in large or small sizes, and can cost thousands or be budget-friendly, at a hundred dollars or less, depending on how much supervision they require. They have a smaller fuel box offset from a larger cooking chamber, which allows you to add fuel without opening the lid where the food sits. Learning how to control the airflow and heat—hotter next to the fuel box—takes some practice, but the results are stellar.

**PELLET SMOKER:** These smokers are often more expensive but are loaded with features and are more automated. They have temperature controls, alarms, and meat probes, and some are Bluetooth-connected, so you can monitor your cook from miles away. The compressed wood pellet fuel is loaded into a hopper, and it's fed through an auger as needed; you just set the time and temperature and the smoker does the rest.

**PROPANE SMOKER:** These are like electric smokers with a handy temperature dial. They use a pellet tray and propane flame to produce the smoke.

# MEXICAN RICE

This is, hands down, some of the best Mexican rice you'll ever eat. Much like Brisket Charro Beans (see page 54), Mexican rice doesn't have to be complicated. My grandma *always* used frozen peas and carrots so that's the way I make it. For the chicken base, you can use powder, but I prefer the congealed, gelatin-like version. Be sure to strain the chipotle peppers before blending them.

2 cups (480 ml) water

4 Roma tomatoes, diced

½ cup (136 g) chipotles in adobo

¼ cup (64 g) tomato paste

2 tablespoons (40 g) chicken base

4 garlic cloves, minced

2 tablespoons (22 g) adobo seasoning

1 tablespoon (10 g) kosher salt

1 teaspoon granulated garlic

1 teaspoon ground black pepper

1 teaspoon ground cumin

3 cups (600 g) jasmine rice

¾ cup (180 ml) canola oil, divided

1 cup (130 g) frozen mixed peas and carrots

1 cup (160 g) diced white onion

2 bay leaves

1. In a blender or food processor, combine the water, tomatoes, chipotles, tomato paste, and chicken base and purée until smooth. Add the minced garlic, adobo seasoning, salt, granulated garlic, pepper, and cumin and pulse to create a slurry.

2. In a large pot over medium heat, fry the rice in ½ cup (120 ml) of the oil for 4 to 5 minutes, stirring constantly, until fragrant. Transfer to a bowl.

3. Add the remaining ¼ (60 ml) oil to the pot and sauté the peas and carrots and onion for 3 to 4 minutes, or until tender.

4. Add the slurry, bay leaves, and fried rice to the vegetables and bring to a simmer. Cover the pot and cook over low heat for 25 to 35 minutes until the rice is cooked and the water has evaporated. Remove the bay leaves, fluff the rice with a fork or wooden spoon, and serve immediately.

# HATCH CHILE CHEDDAR MASHED POTATOES

Cheesy. Tex-Mex. Potatoes. Three things that are awesome enough on their own, but together become an unstoppable force—like watching Captain Planet on a Saturday morning with a bowl of Fruit Loops and too much milk. Speaking of milk, we aren't using any, because HWC is the unsung hero of these potatoes. And its sidekick is hatch chile cheddar, a creamy white cheddar infused with flavorful New Mexican green chiles. I recommend a tablespoon of kosher salt here, but generally speaking, mashed potatoes need lots of butter, salt, and cream, so salt it to taste. Remember, you can always add to, but you can't take it away.

**2 pounds (1 kg) russet potatoes, peeled and cubed**

**1 cup (235 ml) heavy whipping cream**

**6 tablespoons (85 g) unsalted butter**

**1 cup (240 g) hatch chile cheddar cheese, grated, plus more as needed**

**1 tablespoon (10 g) kosher salt**

**1 teaspoon white pepper**

**1 teaspoon granulated garlic**

**1 teaspoon onion powder**

**½ teaspoon Mexican oregano**

1. Place the cubed potatoes in a large pot and cover with water. Bring to a boil over high heat and cook the potatoes for 15 to 18 minutes or until fork tender.

2. Drain the potatoes and pass them through a food mill back into the pot they were boiled in.

3. Add the heavy cream and butter, and fold into the potatoes with a spatula.

4. Stir in the grated cheese until melted and well incorporated.

5. Add the seasonings and stir again to combine well.

6. Garnish with additional grated cheese and serve immediately.

# HANNAH'S GARLIC HABANERO PICKLES

In our earliest barbecue days, my wife and I spent our weekends cooking from our home for pop-up events at local breweries. I smoked the meats on my raggedy 250-gallon (950 L) smoker, sleeping on the couch in 30-minute increments from timer to timer; she would wake up around 5 a.m. to start the sides. The one dish she took the most pride in was her pickles. They're a quick brine pickle that packs a punch, using fresh habaneros and garlic.

5 pounds (2.3 kg) pickling cucumbers
2 cups (320 g) kosher salt, divided
8 cups (1.9 L) water
8 cups (1.9 L) white vinegar
1 cup (200 g) granulated sugar
½ cup (88 g) yellow mustard seeds
10 garlic cloves, minced
1 habanero chile, halved
2 bay leaves
2 tablespoons (17 g) whole black peppercorns
½ cup (32 g) fresh dill

1. Using a food processor with the crinkle-cut attachment, slice the cucumbers into ¼-inch (0.6 cm)-thick slices. Layer the pickles in a large metal bowl, adding ¼ cup (40 g) of salt to each layer as you cut them. Toss the pickles to coat them evenly in the salt, then let them sit for 1 hour. Drain the excess liquid but do not rinse.

2. To create the brine, in a large pot, combine the water, vinegar, 1 cup (160 g) salt, sugar, mustard seeds, garlic, chile, bay leaves, and peppercorns. Bring to a boil.

3. Transfer the strained cucumbers to Mason jars or pickling containers. Evenly divide the fresh dill among the jars.

4. Pour the hot brine into the jars, covering the pickles. Seal the jars while hot and let cool to room temperature. Refrigerate once cool and let sit for 2 to 3 days before serving. Keep refrigerated for up to 12 months.

# SPICY PICKLED RED ONIONS

The perfect accompaniment to Tex-Mex barbecue, these pickled onions cut through the richness of smoked beef, pork, and poultry alike. They're best served atop a flour tortilla or a tostada shell—and you won't be able to pickle them fast enough. Similar to Hannah's Garlic Habanero Pickles (page 61), the onions require a hot brine but generally take only 24 hours to pickle before serving. Be sure to keep the onion peels as they help tremendously with the vibrant purple-pink color you want in a good pickled red onion.

4 cups (960 ml) water

4 cups (960 ml) white vinegar

1 cup (200 g) granulated sugar

6 garlic cloves, minced

¼ cup (40 g) kosher salt

¼ cup (34 g) whole black peppercorns

5 pounds (2.3 kg) red onions, peeled and julienned, peels reserved

1 serrano chile, sliced thinly

1. In a stockpot over medium-high heat, combine the water, vinegar, sugar, garlic, salt, peppercorns, and reserved onion peels (tie the onion peels in a sachet). Bring to a low boil and let boil for 2 to 3 minutes until the sugar and salt dissolve.

2. Evenly divide the onions and sliced serrano among individual Mason jars. Pour the hot brine into the jars, covering the onions and making sure to spoon the garlic and peppercorns over them. Seal the jars and refrigerate for at least 24 hours before serving. Keep refrigerated for up to 12 months.

# CRUNCHY KALE SLAW

Kale isn't exactly the first thing that comes to mind when you think of Tex-Mex—or barbecue for that matter—but this slaw is one of the best accompaniments to smoky, savory meats you can find. The peanuts and pumpkin seeds, or pepitas, give it texture, and the balance of sweet and heat between the green apple and habaneros dances across your palate. The vinaigrette cuts perfectly through fatty, rich brisket on a hot summer day.

## FOR HONEY LIME VINAIGRETTE

**½ cup (120 ml) water**
**¼ cup (60 ml) fresh lime juice**
**Grated zest of 1 lime**
**¼ cup (80 g) honey**
**2 garlic cloves, peeled**
**1 teaspoon kosher salt**
**1 teaspoon ground white pepper**
**½ teaspoon granulated garlic**
**½ teaspoon ground cumin**
**½ cup (120 ml) canola oil or**
  **avocado oil**

## FOR CRUNCH KALE SLAW

**6 cups (402 g) roughly chopped**
  **washed kale**
**½ head red cabbage, julienned**
**1 celery stalk, chopped**
**1 Granny Smith apple, chopped**
**1 cucumber, chopped**
**½ red onion, julienned**
**¼ cup (4 g) fresh cilantro,**
  **chopped**
**½ cup (50 g) chopped scallion,**
  **the green parts**
**1 habanero chile, seeded**
  **and chopped**
**¼ cup (16 g) toasted pumpkin**
  **seeds**
**¼ cup (36 g) chopped peanuts**
**½ cup (75 g) feta cheese**

1. To prepare the vinaigrette, in a blender, combine all the ingredients *except* the oil. Blend on medium speed for 4 to 5 seconds until smooth, then turn the speed to low. With the blender running, slowly pour in the oil to emulsify and thicken the vinaigrette.

2. To assemble the slaw, in a large bowl combine all the slaw ingredients and toss to mix well.

3. Pour the dressing over the slaw and mix to coat and combine. Serve immediately.

# BACON BRAISED CABBAGE

I didn't grow up in a household where cabbage was often—if ever—found on our dinner table, but I came to love it after eating a cabbage roll at an Eastern European restaurant near campus while in college. This recipe is a seasonal dish that works best in fall or the colder months, but is easy to eat anytime because it's just that damn good. I prefer using a thick-cut bacon that's smoked, and adding a little extra garlic when sautéing the bacon.

8 ounces (225 g) bacon, cut into 1-inch (2.5 cm) pieces
1 head green cabbage, halved and cored
2 garlic cloves, minced
2 tablespoons (28 g) unsalted butter
1 teaspoon kosher salt
1 teaspoon ground black pepper
½ teaspoon garlic powder
½ teaspoon onion powder
½ teaspoon smoked paprika

1. In a wok or stockpot over medium-high heat, cook the bacon for 8 to 10 minutes, or until that fat is rendered and the bacon is crispy. Using a slotted spoon, remove the bacon from the fat and set aside, leaving the fat in the pan.

2. Cut the cabbage into 1-inch (2.5 cm) pieces and add to the bacon fat. Cook the cabbage, stirring, for 4 to 5 minutes until it begins to soften. Add the minced garlic and butter. Stir in the salt, pepper, garlic powder, onion powder, and smoked paprika. Continue to cook, stirring, for 3 to 4 minutes, or until the garlic is fragrant. Add the bacon and stir well to incorporate. Remove from the heat and serve immediately.

# BRISKET ESQUITES

Brisket esquites (or elotes) is a dish that perfectly melds "Mexicue" or Tex-Mex cuisine and barbecue. Several barbecue restaurants the state of Texas have adopted "brisket elotes," including mine, and I serve this exact recipe at our stand at Globe Life Field for Texas Rangers fans. It's the perfect balance of savory and spicy—from buttery corn, creamy mayonnaise, the sharpness of cotija cheese, and the heat from your favorite hot sauce.

**4 ounces (55 g) salted butter**

**2 tablespoons (30 ml) canola oil**

**1 pound (454 g) fresh corn kernels**

**1 teaspoon minced garlic**

**½ cup (60 g) mayonnaise**

**6 ounces (115 g) Cotija cheese, grated and divided**

**1 teaspoon kosher salt**

**1 teaspoon ground black pepper**

**8 ounces (115 g) chopped Tex-Mex Smoked Brisket (page 89), or store-bought (warmed up if using leftover brisket)**

**4 tablespoons (30 ml) hot sauce (such as Valentina)**

**2 tablespoons (2 g) chopped fresh cilantro**

**Lime wedges, for garnish**

1. In a skillet over medium-high heat, heat the butter and oil together until melted. Add the corn and let cook, undisturbed, for 1 to 2 minutes to "char." Cook the corn for 3 to 4 minutes longer, stirring, then add the garlic, mayonnaise, half of the Cotija cheese, salt, and pepper. Continuing to cook, folding the mayonnaise in until incorporated, another 1 to 2 minutes.

2. Transfer the corn to a serving bowl and top with the brisket.

3. Sprinkle the remaining Cotija cheese on the corn and drizzle with hot sauce. Garnish with cilantro and lime wedges to serve.

# TATER TOT CASSEROLE

Tater tots. Bacon. Cheddar. Garlic. Butter. These are the ingredients to happiness in life. This is another seasonal recipe that works well in fall and spring, and is incredibly easy to make in advance, if needed. Garnish with scallions or French's crispy fried onion strings for the perfect texture. This dish makes a good amount of casserole for a reason—it's even better when reheated. So, if you don't eat it all (which will be hard not to), you can store it in a baking dish and pop it in the oven to easily reheat it.

**5 pounds (2.3 kg) Tater Tots**

**30 ounces (3 cans) (794 g) diced tomatoes and green chilies (preferably RO-TEL brand)**

**12 ounces (340 g) cream of mushroom soup**

**1 cup (240 g) sour cream**

**1 pound (454 g) shredded cheddar cheese**

**6 ounces (170 g) scallions, green parts, chopped, plus more for garnish**

**4 ounces (115 g) bacon, chopped**

**2 tablespoons (20 g) kosher salt**

**2 tablespoons (12 g) ground black pepper**

**1 tablespoon (10 g) granulated garlic**

**2 ounces (55 g) crispy onion strings**

1. Bake the tots according to the package directions until crispy. Remove from the oven and adjust the oven temperature to 400°F (200°C, or gas mark 6).

2. Coat a 9 × 13-inch (23 × 33 cm) baking dish with nonstick cooking spray.

3. While the tots cook, in a large bowl, whisk together all the wet ingredients along with the cheddar, chopped scallions, bacon, salt, pepper, and granulated garlic.

4. Fold the cooked tots into the wet mixture, then pour the mixture into the prepared baking dish. Bake for 40 minutes until golden brown.

5. Garnish with the crispy onions and scallions. Serve immediately.

# HATCH CHILE CHEDDAR GRITS

There are few things I enjoy more on a chilly day than a warm bowl of grits. This dish takes it to the next level with freshly grated cheddar cheese, and adds a whole new layer of flavor with roasted Hatch chiles. A good friend and neighbor drives to Hatch, New Mexico, once a year, around September, to stock up on chiles during their peak season, then roasts them in his backyard before peeling the skins and vacuum sealing the flesh in bulk for the next 365 days. Use canned green chilies for a similar heat and texture.

4 cups (960 ml) water

4 cups (960 ml) whole milk

2 cups (280 g) white stone-ground grits

2 tablespoons (28 g) unsalted butter

1 tablespoon (10 g) kosher salt

1 teaspoon restaurant-style ground black pepper

1 teaspoon granulated garlic

½ cup (90 g) roasted, peeled, seeded, and chopped Hatch chiles

2 cups (240 g) freshly shredded extra-sharp cheddar cheese

¼ cup (20 g) crumbled cooked bacon

¼ cup (25 g) bias-sliced scallions, green parts

1. In a medium-size saucepan or pot over medium-high heat, bring the water and milk to a gradual boil. Slowly whisk in the grits, then reduce the heat to maintain a simmer. Cook for 15 to 20 minutes, stirring frequently, or until the grits begin to thicken.

2. Stir in the butter until melted. Add the salt, pepper, granulated garlic, and chiles. Stir until incorporated.

3. Mix in the cheddar and continue stirring until the grits are smooth and the cheese is melted. Serve immediately, garnished with bacon and scallions.

# ANCHO AIOLI BRUSSELS SPROUTS

I'll be honest—I didn't invent fried Brussels sprouts, and there are at least 407 recipes for them online, but I haven't seen anyone using ancho aioli on their sprouts, and they're damn good this way. Feel free to fry them in beef tallow or bacon fat for extra flavor, or bake them for a healthier option. It's your life—live your best one.

### FOR BRUSSELS SPROUTS

**1 pound (454 g) Brussels sprouts, trimmed and halved**
**2 tablespoons (30 ml) canola oil**
**1 teaspoon kosher salt**

### FOR ANCHO AIOLI

**1 teaspoon ground black pepper**
**½ cup (120 g) mayonnaise**
**1 tablespoon (15 ml) fresh lime juice**
**Grated zest of 1 lime, plus more for garnish (optional)**
**1 tablespoon (10 g) minced garlic**
**1 teaspoon ancho chile powder**

1. Preheat the oven to 400°F (200°C, or gas mark 6). Line a baking sheet with parchment paper.

2. In a large bowl, toss the sprouts with the oil, salt, and pepper until well combined. Spread the sprouts on the prepared baking sheet. Roast for 25 to 30 minutes, or until tender and slightly charred, stirring once halfway through.

3. While the Brussels sprouts cook, prepare the ancho aioli: In a food processor, combine the mayonnaise, lime juice and zest, garlic, and ancho chile powder. Blend for 6 to 8 seconds until smooth.

4. Serve the Brussels sprouts in a bowl, drizzled with the ancho aioli and garnished with lime zest (if using).

# HATCH CHILE MAC AND CHEESE

My most popular side, and one that has never left the menu since my food trailer days, this Hatch chile mac and cheese has transformed over the years to its glorious, gooey final form that I call "home" today. Cavatappi noodles are best here because of their structural integrity, but you can use macaroni noodles or even penne pasta. If you don't have access to fresh Hatch chiles, use canned green chilies as a substitute, or even roasted poblanos for added flavor.

8 ounces (225 g) dried cavatappi pasta

2 tablespoons (28 g) unsalted butter

⅓ cup (60 g) diced roasted Hatch chiles, plus more for garnish (optional)

3 tablespoons (23.25 g) all-purpose flour

3 cups (720 ml) whole milk

2 cups (240 g) shredded cheddar cheese

1 cup (120 g) shredded American cheese

1 teaspoon kosher salt

½ teaspoon ground black pepper

½ teaspoon granulated garlic

½ teaspoon onion powder

½ teaspoon smoked paprika

Toasted bread crumbs, for garnish (optional)

1. Cook the cavatappi noodles according to the package directions until al dente. Drain and set aside.

2. In a large saucepan over medium heat, melt the butter. Add the Hatch chiles and sauté for 1 to 2 minutes. Whisk in the flour and cook for 1 to 2 minutes, or until the flour begins to thicken and form a paste.

3. Gradually whisk in the milk, making sure lumps do not form. Cook for 3 to 4 minutes until the sauce begins to thicken.

4. Turn the heat to low and gradually add the shredded cheeses. Cook, stirring, until melted.

5. Add the seasonings and cook for 1 to 2 minutes, stirring occasionally.

6. Add the cooked noodles to the cheese sauce, folding them in to combine well.

7. Serve garnished with roasted hatch chiles or toasted bread crumbs (if using).

# AL PASTOR WINGS

These smoked barbecue wings combine the best of both worlds between a traditional Mexican al pastor marinade and crispy tailgate party wings. If you don't have a vacuum sealer to expedite the marinating process, let the wings rest in an airtight container in the refrigerator overnight to really lock in the flavor.

1 cup (240 ml) pineapple juice

¼ cup (60 ml) fresh orange juice

¼ cup (60 ml) white vinegar

2 tablespoons (30 ml) fresh lime juice

2 tablespoons (30 ml) soy sauce

2 tablespoons (44 g) achiote paste

1 tablespoon (14 g) light brown sugar

1 tablespoon (7.5 g) dark chili powder

1 tablespoon (7 g) smoked paprika

1 teaspoon granulated garlic

1 teaspoon onion powder

1 teaspoon dried Mexican oregano

1 teaspoon kosher salt

½ teaspoon ground black pepper

2 pounds (908 g) chicken wings

1 cup (240 ml) reserved marinade, for basting

1 tablespoon (1 g) chopped fresh cilantro

1. In a large bowl, combine the pineapple juice, orange juice, vinegar, lime juice, soy sauce, achiote paste, brown sugar, chili powder, smoked paprika, granulated garlic, onion powder, oregano, salt, and pepper. Whisk to combine. Reserve 1 cup (240 ml) of the marinade for basting.

2. Place the chicken wings in a vacuum-seal bag and pour the remaining marinade over the wings. Vacuum-seal the bag to expedite the marinating process. Refrigerate the al pastor wings for 1 to 2 hours.

3. Preheat a smoker to 275°F (140°C) using pecan or mesquite wood.

4. Remove the wings from the marinade, discard the used marinade, and place them on a wire rack. Set the rack in the smoker nearest the firebox. Smoke the wings for 1 hour, basting with the reserved marinade every 25 to 30 minutes. Cook the wings for 30 to 45 minutes longer to an internal temperature of 165°F (74°C). Transfer to a serving platter and top with any remaining marinade. Garnish with cilantro and serve immediately.

# SERRANO LIME SLAW

Similarly to my Crunchy Kale Slaw (page 65), this recipe has a tangy dressing, but packs a lot more punch with the serrano chiles. It's more of a traditional Tex-Mex slaw, and I opened my food trailer with this as one of our staple sides in 2019.

2 cups (140 g) shredded green cabbage

2 cups (140 g) shredded purple cabbage

½ cup (55 g) shredded carrot

½ cup (58 g) julienned red onion

½ cup (8 g) chopped fresh cilantro

1 serrano chile, thinly sliced

½ cup (120 g) mayonnaise

¼ cup (60 g) sour cream

Grated zest of 1 lime

2 tablespoons (30 ml) fresh lime juice

2 tablespoons (40 g) honey

1 tablespoon (12.5 g) granulated sugar

1 teaspoon minced garlic

½ teaspoon kosher salt, plus more as needed

½ teaspoon ground cumin

½ teaspoon ground white pepper, plus more as needed

½ teaspoon red chili flakes

1. In a large bowl, combine the green and purple cabbages, carrot, onion, cilantro, and serrano. Wearing food-safe gloves, mix well.

2. In a medium-size bowl, combine the remaining ingredients and whisk until smooth. Pour the dressing over the vegetables and mix until combined well. Taste and add more salt and white pepper as needed.

# CHILE
# PEPPERS

Tex-Mex cuisine is known for its heat, from subtle to tongue-tingling, which is created with various chiles in all their forms—fresh, smoked, dried, roasted, and ground. Chile pepper heat is measured on the Scoville scale (SHU), a unit of measurement rating capsaicin—the spicy compound in chiles. The higher the number, the hotter the chile.

There are thousands of chile varieties, but the ones commonly found in Tex-Mex barbecue in order of heat are:

**ANCHO:** These are dried poblano chiles, used both whole and ground. Anchos have a fruity, smoky flavor and mild heat (1,000 to 1,500 SHU).

**POBLANO:** These are dark green with a wide tapering shape and a sweetish, mild flavor (1,000 to 2,000 SHU). They are often stuffed with meat or cheese, breaded, and deep-fried.

**HATCH (GREEN):** Found in the Hatch Valley of New Mexico, these chiles are usually used fresh, canned, or roasted. They are mild (1,500 to 2,500 SHU) with an earthy, almost oniony flavor that becomes sweeter and smoky when roasted.

**HATCH (RED):** These are the ripe versions of green hatch chiles, usually used dried and ground. Red hatch chiles have an earthy flavor and can range in heat (1,000 to 8,000 SHU).

**GUAJILLO:** One of the most commonly used chiles, these are prized for their sweet, fruity, smoky, almost tannic flavor and fairly mild heat (2,500 to 5,000 SHU).

**CHIPOTLE:** These are dried, smoked, ripe, red jalapeños known for their distinct, smoky flavor and mild to moderate heat (2,500 to 8,000 SHU).

**JALAPEÑO:** These can be found fresh, pickled, or canned in most grocery stores. They have a sharp flavor and broad heat range (4,000 to 10,000 SHU).

**SERRANO:** These small red, brown, yellow, or green peppers have a fresh, grassy flavor and a broad range (10,000 to 20,000 SHU).

**CHILE DE ARBOL:** These small bright-red chiles—used fresh, dried, and ground—pack some heat (15,000 to 30,000 SHU).

**HABANERO:** Habaneros are small, lantern-shaped red, yellow, or orange chiles usually sold fresh with serious heat (100,000 to 300,000 SHU).

# GARLIC CHORIZO GREEN BEANS

Green beans have their place solidified in traditional barbecue, but most of the restaurants that serve them tend to jazz up canned green beans with bacon and spices, leaving a mushy, soupy mess with little texture or flavor. This is not that! These green beans are garlicky, spicy, salty, and, most important, have texture! I rotate them seasonally on the sides menu, but they deserve a permanent spot year-round. Once you try them, they'll likely earn a permanent spot in your kitchen, too.

**4 to 5 tablespoons (40 to 50 g) kosher salt, divided**

**1 tablespoon (14 g) light brown sugar**

**1 teaspoon seasoned salt**

**1 teaspoon ground black pepper**

**1 pound (454 g) French green beans (haricots verts), trimmed**

**8 ounces (225 g) Mexican chorizo**

**4 garlic cloves, minced**

**2 tablespoons (28 g) unsalted butter**

I. Fill a medium-size pot halfway with water and place it over high heat. Season the water with 3 to 4 tablespoons (30 to 40 g) of salt. Bring to a boil.

2. While the water heats, in a small bowl, stir together 1 teaspoon kosher salt, brown sugar, seasoned salt, and pepper.

3. Prepare an ice bath in a large bowl.

4. Once the water boils, carefully add the green beans and stir so they're submerged. Boil for 30 seconds, then transfer the beans to the ice bath to shock them and stop the cooking. Drain after 30 to 45 seconds and set aside.

5. Heat a large skillet over medium-high heat. Cook the chorizo in the hot skillet for 3 to 4 minutes, or until fragrant. Add the garlic. Cook the garlic and chorizo for 2 to 3 minutes, stirring.

6. Add the butter and, once it melts, add the green beans and stir so the chorizo coats the beans. Add the seasoning blend and continue to stir. Cook for 1 to 2 minutes longer (do not overcook the green beans). Remove from the heat and serve immediately.

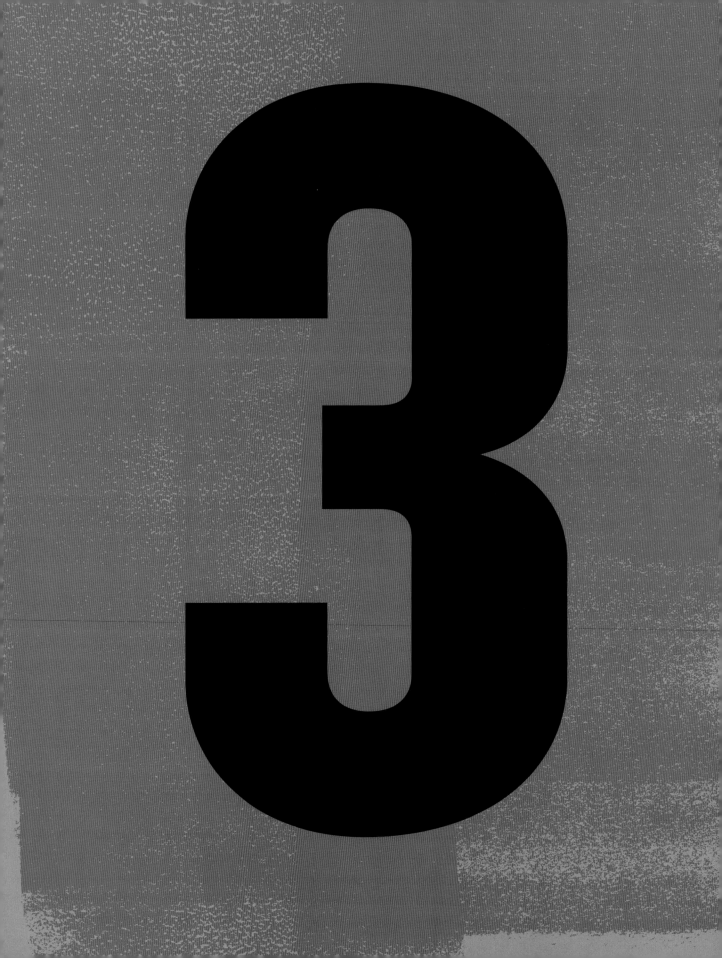

# SMOKED MEATS

## AT HURTADO BARBECUE, I take

a ton of pride in our smoked meats. It all started underneath a tent cooking at a local brewery in Arlington, Texas. At that time, I sourced meats from whatever I could find at Costco. During COVID, supply chain issues made it nearly impossible to find briskets, so I often found myself at local grocery stores with a car full of employees, cash in hand, looking to buy as many briskets as they were willing to sell us (most of which were not Prime grade, and often not even Choice).

The pandemic was a blessing in disguise for my business. It forced me to think outside the box, and birthed creations like the Big Red Barbacoa Tostadas (page 148), mostly because I couldn't find brisket so I had to seek alternative proteins that were available through suppliers.

Even post-COVID, sourcing Prime grade briskets can be a challenge. Less than 3 percent of the nation's beef is graded as Prime, and during the summer months it can be incredibly challenging to find higher-grade beef. However, I use the best quality beef available because no one goes to a steakhouse and asks for a Select rib eye—why would a brisket or beef short rib be any different?

In this chapter, you'll learn exactly how I smoke meats at the restaurants every day, and how to overcome some of the challenges that different proteins present in the pit room.

# TEX-MEX SMOKED BRISKET

Barbecue is a fickle beast when it comes to brisket, and what people determine to be a "good cook." To be honest, barbecue is incredibly subjective, and what one might deem delicious could be seen by anotheras overly smoky, not smoky enough, too tender, or too tough. For me, there's one simple determining factor as to what makes a great brisket—the flat, or the lean part. There's much more forgiveness (and fat) in the point or "moist" part of the brisket, making it easier to cook. The flat, though, is particularly difficult to master because it has less intramuscular fat and, depending on the grade, may have little to no fat at all, making it easier to dry out.

But after cooking thousands of briskets, I've found a few checks and balances to ensure both the point and the flat turn out smoky, tender, and, most important, moist. Pro tip: You'll know your briskets are done when the butcher paper is completely saturated and has a "nutty," or even sweet chocolate, smell to it.

---

**1 (12- to 15-pound, or 5.4 to 8.8 kg) Prime grade packer brisket**

**8 ounces (225 g) yellow mustard**

**2 ounces (60 ml) pickle juice**

**1½ cups (about 340 g) Hurtado Beef Blend (page 28)**

**1 cup (136 g) #30 coarse-ground black pepper**

**I.** Preheat a smoker to 180°F (82°C). If cooking on an offset smoker, create a "Lincoln log" fire with 4 or 5 splits.

**2.** Start to trim the brisket by removing the hard deckle fat underneath. I typically use a slicing knife (not serrated) to achieve cleaner cuts versus a boning knife. The hard fat is usually around 2½ x 4 inches (6.5 cm x 10 cm) in size and lies underneath the "point" or fatty part of the brisket. In one smooth slicing motion, cut it off the brisket without cutting too far into the meat.

**3.** Remove the "mohawk" from the top of the brisket (the part with the fat cap). This is on the opposite side of where you just removed the hard deckle fat. Contrary to the deckle fat, the mohawk is more soft and pillowy, full of marbled protein from the point of the brisket, and can be used for burnt ends, or even barbacoa. The mohawk can be identified by where it sits on the brisket—on top of the point (the fatty part), and on either side, depending on whether it's a left or right brisket (from the left or right side of the cow). It may already have a "mohawk" shape to it, but you can exaggerate it by pinching the meat between your thumb, index and middle finger to see how much you need to remove. Again, using your slicing knife, remove the mohawk in one smooth slicing motion. The reason for removing this is so it doesn't burn up during the cooking process, and it makes your brisket more aerodynamic for a more consistent cook.

**CONTINUED ➨➨**

4. Using a boning knife or filet knife, round the edges of the brisket flat (the lean part) and carefully remove any additional fat from the cap, leaving roughly ¼ inch (0.6 cm) of soft, pillowy fat across the flat and point.

5. In a squeeze bottle, combine the mustard and pickle juice. Cover and shake to combine well. Squeeze a thin line of mustard across the bottom side of the brisket, then gently massage it all over. Do the same to the top of the brisket.

6. Starting with the bottom part (not the side with the fat cap), sprinkle the black pepper across the brisket first. This helps create a stellar bark and helps "catch" the beef rub in between the pepper so it doesn't rub off easily during the cooking process. Liberally season the brisket with the beef blend until all sides are covered.

7. Flip to where the fat side faces upward and repeat.

8. Place the brisket in the smoker, fat-side up, with the point facing the firebox.

9. At this point, focus on fire management. Do not open the cooking chamber until the 4- to 6-hour mark. This will help maintain temperature control and create a more even cook.

10. After 4 hours at 180°F (82°C), gradually increase the temperature to 250°F (120°C). Keep the fire at 250°F (120°C) until the 10-hour mark, or until the brisket reaches an internal temperature of 185°F (85°C) between the point and the flat.

11. Once the bark is set (does not rub off easily when you touch it), wrap the brisket tightly with butcher paper. Place the brisket back onto the smoker with the flat facing the firebox (the opposite of how we began) and cook for 2 to 3 hours longer, or until the flat reaches an internal temperature of 205°F (96°C).

12. Begin feeling the bottom of the brisket to ensure it's "soft" and probe the sides—they should feel like butter. When done, pull the brisket and let it rest in an oven or warmer set on low until ready to serve.

13. To slice the brisket, I like to start on the lean side (the flat) and cut the first portion about 1¼-inch (3 cm) thick from the edge. Then, I take those pieces and cut them crossways 3 to 4 times for burnt ends.

14. Then, cut pencil-thick slices (about ¼-inch [0.6 cm]) of lean brisket, focusing on consistent thickness in your slices. The brisket should drape over your finger without falling apart, but easily pull apart without much effort.

15. Once you've cut roughly half of the brisket, you should see the grain in the meat start to change directions, meaning you're getting close to the fatty part. Since you want to always cut against the grain, turn the brisket 180 degrees and begin slicing the fatty section the opposite direction. This is the "point" of the brisket and will have more savory, decadent slices of brisket.

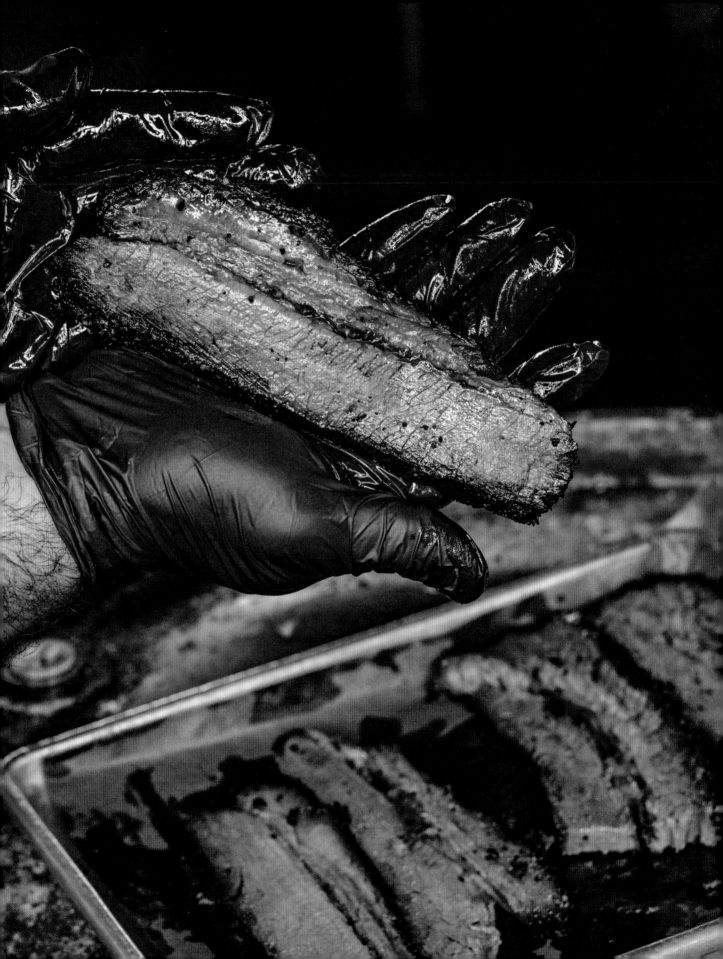

# TEXAS PORK RIBS

Pork ribs are, perhaps, the one protein that gets me the most excited about Texas barbecue. Yes, even more than brisket. Pork ribs give you identity. They provide a canvas for creativity. I firmly believe that Dayne Weaver makes some of the best pork ribs in the state of Texas. When I first had Dayne's ribs (from Dayne's Craft Barbecue in Aledo, Texas), I knew that he had something special. Dayne's ribs have the perfect "bite" and a slight sweetness with a beautiful reddish-mahogany color achieved with a clean fire and his signature rib glaze. They've gotten better every time I've eaten them . . .

But the ribs that inspire me the most belong to Esaul Ramos from 2M Smokehouse in San Antonio. I first visited Esaul in 2019 when I was getting started in barbecue, and was amazed at the quality and attention to detail of every protein he served. The pork ribs, in my opinion, were one of the single most memorable bites of barbecue I've ever had. The bark was similar to a brisket, and with an incredible glaze that hits your tongue when you first bite into the rib. They were cooked to perfection, leaving just enough "bite" so the ribs didn't fall off the bone, but were tender as a mother's touch. I'm not sure I've had a better rib in Texas barbecue, and I've been chasing those ribs since 2019.

When it comes to pork ribs, you have options:

**Full spare ribs:** These require the most prep work, but yield the best "Texas-size" results. These ribs come from the pig's belly and have the most succulent meat, next to baby back ribs. This is what I use in my restaurants and what I prefer to cook at home. Use the trimmings for rib tips or in Brisket Charro Beans (page 54).

**St. Louis–style ribs:** Most places I know of in Texas serve this cut of pork ribs, which is essentially a rack of spare ribs trimmed to a more manageable, uniform size. Typically used in competitions, St. Louis ribs cook faster and yield a more consistent result because the ribs are usually the same size and shape. Joe from Zavala's Barbecue in Grand Prairie, Texas, does an incredible job with these ribs and focuses on the meat rather than highlighting rubs or a sauce.

**Baby back ribs:** Contrary to the full spare ribs or St. Louis ribs, baby back ribs come from the loin area of the pig and have more lean meat. They cook quickly, similar to St. Louis ribs, but have a totally different flavor profile and texture than spare ribs. I really enjoy grilling and saucing baby back ribs over an open flame as opposed to smoking them.

---

1 rack full spare pork ribs

1 cup (about 225 g) Hurtado Pork Blend (page 29)

Apple cider vinegar, for spritzing

1 cup (240 ml) Original Rib Glaze (page 37)

1. Preheat a smoker to 250°F (120°C).

2. Trim the pork ribs. Remove the chine bone (the backbone) with a boning knife, then remove the skirt from the back of the ribs. Remove the last bone from the tail end of the ribs, as it will typically fall out anyway. Make sure all sides of the ribs are even and somewhat "rounded" instead of square.

3. Season the ribs with the pork blend on the back side first, making sure to cover the sides as well. Flip the ribs and season the top last, ensuring an even coat from end to end. Place the ribs in the smoker with the "top" facing the firebox.

4. Control your fire temperature from between 250°F and 275°F (120°C and 140°C) and cook for 4 hours, spritzing the ribs with vinegar every 45 minutes. This is critical to create that "mahogany" color. Open the cooking chamber door only long enough to quickly spritz the ribs, then shut it immediately so as not to lose any heat. After 4 hours, the ribs should have a bark that doesn't rub off easily and the back side of the ribs should have "pulled back" about ¼ inch (0.6 cm) from the bone. Remove the ribs from the heat.

5. Tear an aluminum foil sheet roughly 4 inches (10 cm) longer than the ribs on each side. Drizzle the glaze onto the foil in an area about the same size as the ribs. Place the ribs on the foil, meat-side down, and tightly fold the top and bottom of the foil over the ribs, then fold over the sides tightly. Put the ribs back in the smoker with the "bottom" of the ribs (where the bones have pulled back from and are exposed) facing the firebox, meat-side down, for 1 hour at 275°F (140°C).

6. Check the ribs for doneness by carefully unwrapping them and holding them in the middle of the rack. They should fold over your hand without breaking, but the fat on top should start to split. The top of the ribs should be soft, and the meat between the bones should feel pillowy without much resistance when you push against it.

7. When the ribs feel done, place them back in the foil until ready to serve. Slice the rack meat-side down for the easiest, cleanest cuts.

# BARBACOA CON PAPAS

When you think of barbacoa, your mind probably goes straight to tacos—slow-cooked beef cheek piled on warm, pillowy flour tortillas, topped with salsa verde or cilantro and onion. What you don't think of is a dish that could be served at a celebrity dinner, or in a Michelin-starred restaurant, which is exactly what this is. I most recently served barbacoa con papas at Taylor Sheridan's ranch house for a dinner where guests wanted something beyond traditional barbecue, which is what we do best. The things I love most about this dish are the surprising heat from the chili oil, the complexity of flavors from the velvety elote "velouté," and texture from the potatoes. Kick this dish up a notch by frying the potatoes in beef tallow after boiling them for even more texture and flavor.

## FOR BEEF CHEEKS
1 pound (454 g) beef cheeks, trimmed
¼ cup (34 g) coarse-ground black pepper
2 tablespoons (20 g) kosher salt
1 tablespoon (7 g) ground cumin
1 tablespoon (10 g) granulated garlic
1 teaspoon cayenne pepper
1 teaspoon dried Mexican oregano
8 cups (1.9 L) beef stock

## FOR PAPAS Y CHORIZO
1 pound (454 g) petite potatoes, washed and scrubbed
8 ounces (225 g) Mexican chorizo
2 ounces (55 g) epazote
2 to 3 tablespoons (17 to 25.5 g) reserved beef seasoning

## FOR ESQUITES VELOUTÉ
3 tablespoons (45 ml) canola oil, plus ½ cup (120 ml)
12 ounces (340 g) fresh corn kernels
4 ounces (115 g) mayonnaise
2 ounces (55 g) Cotija cheese, grated
¼ cup (4 g) chopped fresh cilantro
Kosher salt

## FOR CHILI OIL
½ cup (120 ml) canola oil
2 tablespoons (20 g) minced garlic
1 tablespoon (6 g) red chili flakes

## FOR CREMA
8 ounces (225 g) Mexican crema
1 garlic clove, minced
1 tablespoon (1 g) chopped fresh cilantro

CONTINUED ▶▶

1. Preheat a smoker to 250°F (120°C).

2. To prepare the beef cheeks, trim the beef, removing any hard cartilage or fat, as well as any sinew, or connective tissue.

3. In a shaker bottle, combine the black pepper, salt, cumin, granulated garlic, cayenne, and oregano. Liberally season the beef cheeks on all sides with the spices and reserve any remaining seasoning. Place the beef cheeks in the smoker for 4 hours, or until they reach an internal temperature of 165°F (74°C). Transfer them to a 4-inch (10 cm)-deep baking dish (12 × 20-inch, or 30 × 50 cm) and add the stock. Wrap the pan tightly with aluminum foil and place it back in the smoker for about 2½ hours, or until the meat feels tender when probed and reaches an internal temperature of about 200°F (93°C). Remove from the smoker and let cool to 160°F (71°C) internal in the broth to keep moist.

4. To prepare the papas y chorizo, bring a large pot of water to a boil over high heat. Add the potatoes and boil for 8 to 10 minutes until al dente (not fully cooked). Drain and pat dry.

5. In a cast-iron skillet over medium-high heat, cook the chorizo for 5 to 7 minutes until cooked through, stirring with a wooden spoon or spatula. Add the potatoes, epazote, and 2 to 3 tablespoons (17 to 25.5 g) of the reserved beef cheek seasoning and cook for 3 to 4 minutes, stirring occasionally, until the potatoes are fork-tender on the inside and crispy on the outside.

6. To prepare the esquites velouté soup, in a saucepan over medium-high heat, heat 3 tablespoons (45 ml) of the oil until hot. Add the corn and cook for 4 to 5 minutes, stirring constantly. Stir in the mayonnaise, Cotija cheese, and cilantro until the mayonnaise is incorporated. Cook for 4 to 5 minutes until the corn is translucent and tender, then season to taste with salt. Carefully transfer the corn mixture to a blender. While blending on medium speed, slowly pour in the remaining ½ cup (120 ml) of oil, emulsifying until the mixture is smooth and velvety. Add salt to taste.

7. To prepare the chili oil, in a small saucepan over medium heat, heat the canola oil until hot.

8. In a ramekin, combine the minced garlic and red chili flakes. Carefully pour the hot oil over them. Let cool.

9. To prepare the crema, in a blender, combine the Mexican crema, garlic, and cilantro. Pulse 2 to 3 times until smooth. Transfer to a squeeze bottle and set aside.

10. To plate, for each serving, ladle 1 cup (240 ml) of the corn soup into a bowl. Spoon some of the potatoes and chorizo on the soup, making sure to include epazote leaves. Drizzle the crema across the potatoes and chorizo.

11. Carefully slice the beef cheek into ½-inch (1 cm) thick slices and lay 2 pieces on the potatoes.

12. Finish with 1 teaspoon of the chili oil drizzled on the beef.

# PORK BELLY BURNT ENDS

Pork belly is another protein that offers a blank canvas for backyard barbecuers and professional pitmasters alike to create a masterpiece that could be savory, sweet, spicy, or all of the above. I've done breakfast burnt ends tossed with Cinnamon Toast Crunch, and have even smoked bulgogi burnt ends for an Asian twist on tacos. In north Texas, bacon burnt ends were made popular most notably by Travis and Emma Heim of Heim Barbecue, and have since been added to barbecue menus across the state. My version of pork belly burnt ends is hard to mess up, and is a solid method for adding your own spin to what works best for your family.

**5 pounds (2.3 kg) raw, skinless pork belly**
**½ cup (about 115 g) Hurtado Pork Blend (page 29)**
**Apple cider vinegar, for spritzing**
**1 cup (320 g) honey**
**½ cup (120 g) packed light brown sugar**
**½ cup (120 ml) My Sweet Sauce (page 33)**
**6 tablespoons (84 g) unsalted butter, cut into 6 portions**

1. Preheat a smoker to 250°F (120°C).

2. Trim the pork belly into 1¼-inch (3 cm) cubes and season with pork blend on all sides. Place the pork belly on a wire rack set on a sheet pan, making sure the cubes are not touching so they "bark" on all sides evenly. Place the sheet pan in the smoker and smoke the pork belly for 3½ to 4 hours, spritzing every hour with apple cider vinegar. The pork will begin to have a mahogany color and the fat should start rendering on top.

3. While the pork smokes, in a medium-size bowl, whisk the honey, brown sugar, and sweet sauce until smooth.

4. Transfer the burnt ends to a 9 × 13-inch (23 × 33 cm) baking dish or aluminum foil pan and drizzle the honey barbecue glaze on top. Toss to coat evenly.

5. Scatter the butter pieces over the burnt ends and wrap the pan tightly with foil. Place the ends back in the smoker for 1½ to 2 hours longer, or until the burnt ends reach an internal temperature of 195°F (90.5°C). They should feel "pillowy" and have very little resistance when pressed between your thumb and index finger.

6. Remove from the smoker and toss again before serving.

# BIG RED BARBACOA

Big Red and barbacoa go together like peanut butter and jelly. Like Selena and Corpus Christi or San Antonio and the Riverwalk. The sweet creaminess from Big Red soda and the smoky saltiness of braised beef cheeks are a match made in south Texas heaven. From the Rio Grande Valley through greater San Antonio, Big Red and barbacoa have been a tradition at local Mexican restaurants and taquerias for decades. There's even an annual Big Red barbacoa festival in San Antonio that highlights local vendors and unique dishes that feature the soda-braised beef. For us, beef cheek has had many applications. Barbacoa is so versatile, I've used it to make everything from tostadas and tortas to Mexican boudin sausage. Contrary to brisket, beef cheeks take way less time to cook and are the perfect alternative for backyard pitmasters who want something a little different (and a whole lot tastier).

---

**2 pounds (908 g) beef cheeks**

**1 cup (about 225 g) Hurtado Beef Blend (page 28)**

**1 cup (115 g) julienned white onion**

**2 cups (480 ml) Big Red soda**

**2 cups (480 ml) beef stock**

1. Preheat a smoker to 225°F (107°C).

2. Trim the beef cheeks, removing any "hard" cartilage or sinew. Season the cheeks liberally with beef blend on all sides. Place the beef cheeks in the smoker for 4½ to 5 hours. Maintain the fire between 225°F and 250°F (107°C and 120°C). Cook the beef until it reaches an internal temperature between 180°F and 185°F (82°C and 85°C). The cheeks should have a peppery bark that does not rub off easily.

3. Remove the cheeks from the smoker. Spread the onion along the bottom of a 9 × 13-inch (23 × 33 cm) baking dish, then top with the beef cheeks.

4. Pour the soda and stock into the baking dish (not over the cheeks). The liquid should cover about 1 inch (2.5 cm) of the beef cheeks. Cover the pan tightly with aluminum foil and return it to the smoker at 275°F to 300°F (140°C to 150°C). Cook for 2 to 2½ hours longer until the cheeks register an internal temperature between 200°F and 205°F (93°C and 96°C). They should be soft and pillowy to the touch. Remove from the heat.

5. Serve the barbacoa sliced, or chopped for tacos, nachos, tostadas, quesadillas, and more. If chopping, work the beef cheeks with your hand to shred the meat first, then chop coarsely, incorporating the onion and remaining braising liquid (½ cup, or 120 ml, at a time) to retain moisture in the meat.

# SMOKED TURKEY BREAST

Turkey is, hands down, the most underrated protein in Texas barbecue. It's simple to make but easy to overcook and dry out. My smoked turkey breast recipe starts with boneless turkey breast lobes that are not brined, but seasoned simply with my poultry blend for a citrusy kick that works well with post oak. Most people think poultry has to be cooked to 165°F (74°C), but there's a pasteurization table or, as I like to call it, a juiciness periodic table, you can follow to ensure maximum flavor without getting your friends and family sick from undercooked poultry. Ideally, poultry only has to reach 150°F (65°C) for 52 seconds to kill any harmful bacteria and be deemed safe for consumption. I like to take my turkey breast to 155°F (68°C) for 30 seconds. This creates some of the juiciest turkey breast imaginable, with the perfect amount of smoke, citrus, and savoriness from the butter.

---

1 (4- to 5-pound, or 1.8 to 2.3 kg) boneless, skinless turkey breast

½ cup (about 115 g) Hurtado Poultry Blend (page 30)

1 cup (240 ml) water

1 cup (240 ml) apple cider vinegar

2 tablespoons (28 g) salted butter

1. Preheat a smoker to 250°F (120°C).

2. Season the turkey breast liberally with poultry blend on all sides. Place the turkey breast in the smoker (breast-side up) for 2 hours.

3. Focus on maintaining the temperature between 250°F and 275°F (120°C and 140°C).

4. In a spray bottle, combine the water and vinegar.

5. After 2 hours, begin spritzing the turkey breast with the vinegar mixture every 30 to 45 minutes. Continue to cook for 2½ to 3 hours longer, spritzing according to schedule, until the turkey breast reaches an internal temperature of 155°F (68°C). Remove from the heat.

6. Place the butter on top of the turkey breast and wrap it tightly with foil to prevent oxidization. Hold in the oven at 155°F (63°C) until ready to serve.

7. Slice in ¼-inch thick slices, using a serrated slicing knife for best results.

# "HEIM HAMMER" SMOKED BEEF SHANK

Smoking a beef shank the size of Texas is something you might not do on a regular basis, but it's a great dish for tailgate parties or birthdays. Heck, I'd smoke one just because. I started selling these as a shareable platter during the Texas Rangers' play-off run in 2023, then launched the "Heim Hammer," named after our All-Star catcher, Jonah Heim, at my stand in the ballpark during the World Series. This is one of those meats that's hard to overcook, but easy to not smoke quite long enough, so let it go, even if it's beyond where you'd normally take beef on a smoker. You can use your favorite barbecue sauce to glaze the beef shank, and even have a taco party afterward, as long as you're sharing with friends.

---

**1 (4- to 6-pound, or 1.8 to 2.7 kg) beef shank**

**¼ cup (44 g) yellow mustard**

**1 cup (about 225 g) Hurtado Beef Blend (page 28)**

**1 cup (240 ml) Original Rib Glaze (page 37)**

**Tortillas, for serving (optional)**

1. Preheat a smoker to 225°F (107°C) using pecan or post oak wood.

2. Slather the beef with the mustard and season it liberally with the beef blend. Stand the beef, shin bone-up, in the smoker and cook for 5 to 6 hours until the bark begins to set and doesn't rub off easily. Probe the beef. Once it reaches an internal temperature between 185°F and 190°F (85°C and 88°C), remove it from the heat and place on two 12-inch (30 cm) square aluminum foil sheets.

3. Pour the rib glaze all over the beef and wrap the foil upward, covering the meat but leaving the bone exposed. Return to the smoker for 1 to 2 hours at 250°F (120°C), or until the beef shin reaches an internal temperature between 205°F and 208°F (96°C and 98°C). Remove from the smoker and discard the foil. Serve immediately with tortillas to create a DIY taco bar or eat it off the bone like a boss.

# TEXAS BEEF RIBS

Like pork ribs, beef ribs come in different sizes and cuts that can be used for different styles of cooking and various recipes. You can use beef back ribs, which have less meat and fat, but are full of flavor. There's also chuck short ribs (the first to fifth ribs), most commonly used for braising or low and slow cooking methods. But in Texas we do everything bigger, so we use the plate short ribs (the sixth to tenth ribs), most commonly called "dino ribs." These are typically sold in sets of three bones to a plate, and are 10 to 12 inches (24 to 30 cm) in length. They contain the most succulent, fatty meat and are often referred to as the Cadillac of Texas barbecue. For my beef ribs, I don't remove the membrane because it helps hold the rib together when slicing. And I much prefer to hit our ribs with black pepper first (before the beef blend) to create a stellar bark.

**1 (4- to 5-pound, or 1.8 to 2.3 kg) plate short rib rack**
**¼ cup (44 g) yellow mustard**
**½ cup (96 g) ground black pepper**
**½ cup (about 115 g) Hurtado Beef Blend (page 28)**
**Apple cider vinegar, for spritzing**

1. Preheat a smoker to 180°F (82°C).

2. I do not trim beef ribs, but remove any pieces of hard bone sticking out. Slather the ribs all over with mustard. Season liberally all over with the pepper, then season with the beef blend—do not season the bottom of the plate ribs. Place the ribs in the smoker with the "top" of the ribs, or larger section of the plate, facing the firebox. Cook for 2 hours, then increase the heat to 250°F (120°C) and begin spritzing with vinegar every hour for 4 more hours.

3. After 6 hours, begin probing the ribs. Once they reach an internal temperature between 180°F and 185°F (82°C and 85°C), wrap them tightly with butcher paper sprayed with vinegar to help with pliability.

4. Return the wrapped ribs to the smoker and cook for 1 to 2 hours longer, or until the ribs probe like butter. They should read somewhere between 200°F and 205°F (93°C and 96°C) when done.

5. Rest the beef ribs until they read 155°F (68°C), then slice and serve immediately.

# SMOKED & FRIED QUAIL

One of the dishes I remember eating while growing up was cooked hot and fast over a campfire fueled by mesquite wood at our family's ranch near Brownwood, Texas. My dad and grandpa loved eating quail, and would often bring a pack of semiboneless quail when they could find it at the local butcher. Quail is one of those sleeper proteins that has incredible flavor with little to no gaminess, and doesn't take much effort to make it really good. You don't have to fry it, but I like the way the skin crisps up after a few seconds in hot oil after being smoked.

**1 teaspoon kosher salt, plus more as needed**

**½ teaspoon restaurant-style ground black pepper**

**½ teaspoon granulated garlic**

**½ teaspoon light chili powder**

**¼ teaspoon ground cumin**

**¼ teaspoon dried Mexican oregano**

**1 pound (454 g) semiboneless quail**

**½ cup (62 g) all-purpose flour**

**4 cups (960 ml) canola oil**

**1.** Preheat a smoker to 250°F (120°C) using pecan or mesquite wood.

**2.** In a small bowl, stir together the spices. Reserve 1 teaspoon (5 g) for the flour dredge. With the remaining spices, season the quail. Place the quail in the smoker and cook for 45 minutes to 1 hour, or until it reaches an internal temperature of 160°F (71°C). Remove the quail from the smoker.

**3.** In another small bowl, combine the reserved spices and the flour and mix well with a fork. Lightly coat the quail on all sides with the seasoned flour.

**4.** In a medium-size saucepan over medium-high, heat the oil to 350°F (180°C).

**5.** Carefully, place the quail into the hot oil and cook for 1 to 2 minutes or until golden brown. Transfer to a wire rack and season with salt. Serve immediately.

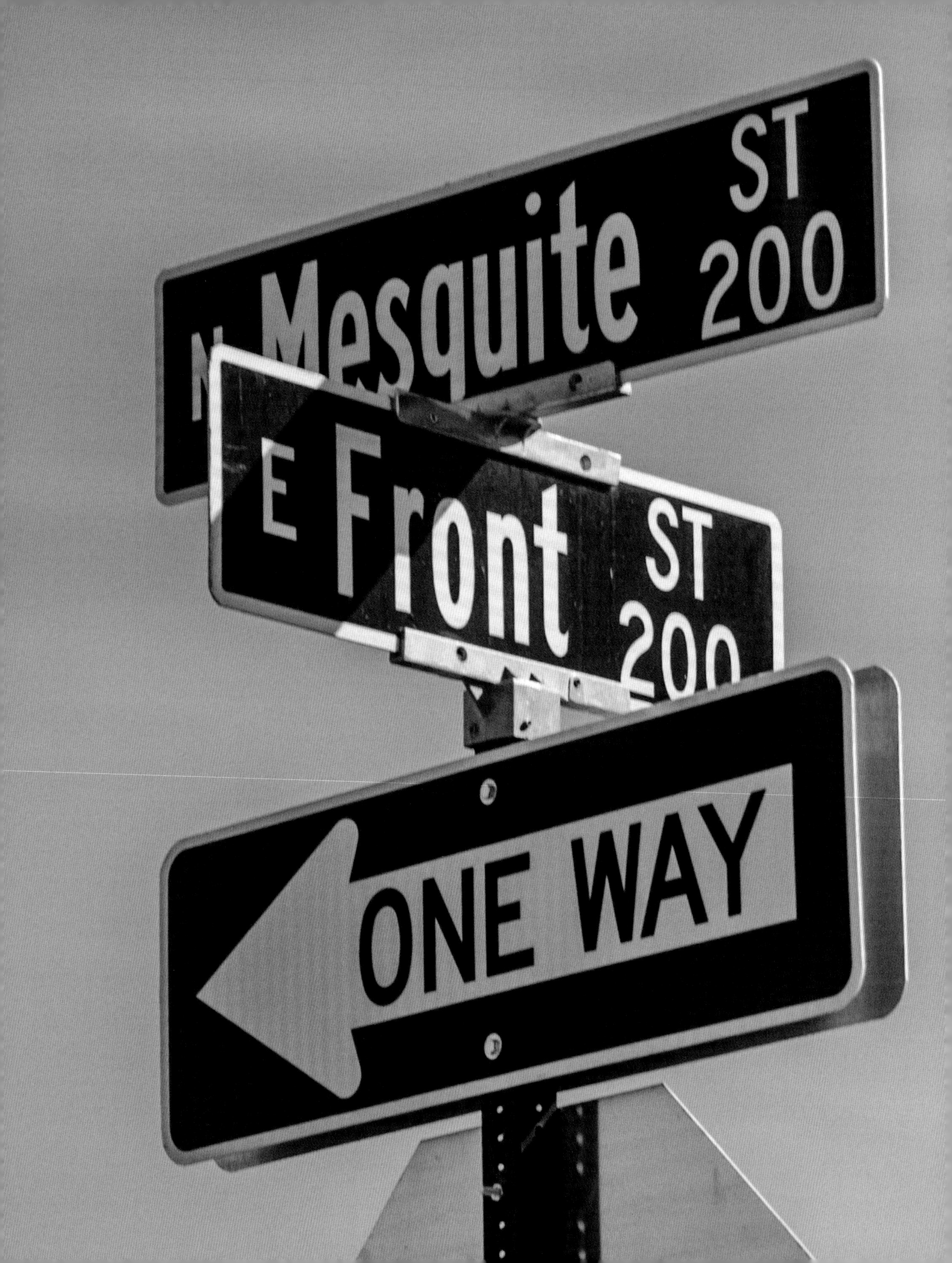
N Mesquite ST 200
E Front ST 200
ONE WAY

# TEX-MEX PULLED PORK

Pork shoulder is one of those meats that's incredibly versatile and relatively inexpensive, but often overlooked or an afterthought on Texas barbecue menus. What I love most about this dish is how well it works with the heat from the spicy mustard. I prefer pulled pork in a warm tortilla, but you can also use it in salads, enchiladas, on a tostada, or even in flautas.

1 cup (240 ml) apple cider vinegar

1 cup (240 ml) water

1 tablespoon (10 g) kosher salt

1 tablespoon (8.5 g) restaurant-style ground black pepper

1 tablespoon (7.5 g) dark chili powder

1 teaspoon smoked paprika

1 teaspoon granulated garlic

1 teaspoon ground cumin

1 teaspoon dried Mexican oregano

1 4- to 5-pound (1.8 to 2.3 kg) bone-in pork shoulder

¼ cup (60 ml) hot sauce (such as Valentina)

1 cup (240 ml) Aztec Gold Mustard Sauce (page 34)

1. Preheat a smoker to 250°F (120°C).

2. In a spray bottle, combine the vinegar and water. Set aside.

3. In a small bowl, stir together the spices. Slather the pork with the hot sauce, then season the pork liberally on all sides with the spices. Place the pork shoulder in the smoker, with a water pan nearest the firebox and the pork shoulder closer to the stack. Cook for 5½ to 6 hours. After 2 hours, begin spritzing with the vinegar-water mixture every 30 minutes.

4. Maintain the heat between 250°F and 275°F (120°C and 140°C).

5. After about 6 hours, probe the pork shoulder. It should be a mahogany color and the fat should look like it's starting to bubble or render on top. Once the pork shoulder reaches an internal temperature of 180°F (82°C), wrap it tightly in aluminum foil, then return it to the smoker for 1 to 2 hours. When the pork shoulder reaches an internal temperature between 200°F and 203°F (93°C and 95°C) and probes like butter, remove it from the smoker and let cool to between 155°F and 160°F (68°C and 71°C).

6. Place the pork shoulder in a large bowl and remove the foil. Remove the bone and use it to shred the pork shoulder. Add the mustard sauce to the pulled pork and mix well by hand to combine. Serve immediately.

# HOW TO
# REHEAT BARBECUE

Once your barbecue drops below 140°F (60°C) (safe temperature), you must eat or refrigerate it within two hours. If the environmental temperature is 90°F or above, this safe zone drops to one hour. Transfer the leftover barbecue to shallow containers so it chills faster, and store it in the refrigerator for three to four days or the freezer for three months. Place the leftovers in airtight containers or sealed freezer bags with as much air pressed out as possible. If the meat is vacuum-sealed, it will keep in the freezer for up to two years.

When it is time to reheat, defrost the barbecue in the refrigerator overnight if it is frozen. Don't reheat food more than once because this increases the risk of bacterial growth.

The best way to reheat your leftovers is the sous vide method. If your meat is vacuum-packed, you can leave it right in the bag, or you can place the meat in a sealable plastic bag with the air pressed out and sealed. Fill a pot large enough to hold the bag about half full of water and bring it to a simmer—about 175°F (80°C)—on the stove. Clip a temperature probe to the pot's side to ensure the water stays to temperature. Add the bag and heat to an internal temperature of 165°F (74°C) for food safety. If in a sealed freezer bag, check the internal temperature occasionally with a probe or laser thermometer gun. It will take about 15 to 20 minutes to reheat. Remove the bag from the pot and serve up your barbecue with any juices from the bag.

If using a conventional oven, preheat the oven to 300°F (150°C, gas mark 2) degrees and remove the barbecue from its bag or container. Wrap the meat or poultry in foil or place it in a shallow baking dish, add ½ cup (120 ml) of water, and cover it with foil. Reheat the food to a minimum internal temperature of 165°F (74°C), checking with a probe occasionally. If reheating a whole brisket, leave it wrapped in butcher paper and place it on a sheet pan. I generally like to reheat brisket to 145°F to 150°F (63°C to 66°C) internal, so as to not overcook the brisket.

# MEXICAN HOT CHICKEN

This one's for all the spice lovers who want to sweat and swear after a few bites of their barbecue. I first made this spicy half chicken while cooking out of our food trailer in 2019 because I didn't have anything with real "heat" on the menu. It has transformed over the years to where we use my buddy Wes Wicker's Big Wicks "Fuego" glaze on the chicken, which includes mesquite-smoked jalapeños and serrano chiles. If you can't find this online, blend your favorite barbecue sauce with mesquite-smoked peppers to replicate a similar heat profile in your chicken glaze. Note that this recipe is HOT and not intended for children or people who (as my daughter says) "don't like spicy!"

---

**1 whole chicken**
**1 tablespoon (10 g) kosher salt**
**1 tablespoon (8.5 g) restaurant-style ground black pepper**
**1 tablespoon (7.5 g) dark chili powder**
**1 tablespoon (5 g) cayenne pepper**
**1 teaspoon granulated garlic**
**1 teaspoon ground cumin**
**1 teaspoon dried Mexican oregano**
**1 cup (240 ml) Big Wicks Fuego glaze**

1. Preheat a smoker to 275°F (140°C) using pecan or mesquite wood.

2. Spatchcock the chicken using sharp kitchen shears to cut down each side of the backbone. Remove the backbone and save it for chicken stock later. Flip the chicken breast-side up, and push down firmly on the breast with the heel of your hand to break the breastbone. Slice down the middle of the breast to evenly cut through the bones and cartilage until the chicken is cut in two halves.

3. In a small bowl, stir together the dry ingredients and season both sides of the chicken halves liberally with the spices. Place the chicken halves in the smoker for 1½ to 2 hours, or until the internal temperature reaches 165°F (74°C) in the breasts and thighs. Maintain the smoker temperature between 275°F and 300°F (140°C and 150°C).

4. Brush the glaze onto the chicken halves and let them tack up in the smoker for 5 to 10 minutes longer.

5. Cut the chicken halves into quarters and serve immediately.

# DIRECT HEAT PORK STEAK

The best pork steak I ever had came from a weekend getaway at Snow's BBQ in Lexington, Texas. Ms. Tootsie Tomanetz, the legendary female pitmaster at Snow's, uses an incredible approach to cooking pork steaks that starts with direct heat over hot coals, and lots of homemade mop sauce. The perfect pork steak should be tender like a rib eye and have lots of smoke flavor and a hint of sweet and tangy from the mop sauce or spritz. Using a bone-in pork shoulder presents the most flavor, but if you don't have a local butcher to cut your steaks, substitute a boneless pork shoulder cut into similar-size steaks.

1 4- to 5-pound (1.8 to 2.3 kg) **bone-in pork shoulder, cut into 1-inch (2.5 cm) steaks**
1 cup (about 225 g) Hurtado Pork Blend (page 29)
1 cup (240 ml) My Sweet Sauce (page 33)
½ cup (120 ml) water
½ cup (120 ml) apple cider vinegar

1. Preheat a smoker to 250°F (120°C) using pecan or post oak wood.

2. Season the pork steaks liberally with the pork blend on both sides. Place the pork steaks in the smoker and cook for 3 to 4 hours. Maintain the fire at 250°F to 275°F (120°C to 140°C).

3. In a medium-size bowl, whisk the sweet sauce, water, and vinegar to make a mop sauce.

4. After the third hour in the smoker, begin mopping the pork steaks with a brush or mop every 30 minutes. Continue to cook for 1 to 2 hours until the pork steaks reach an internal temperature between 185°F and 190°F (85°C and 88°C). Remove from the heat and serve immediately.

# CHRISTMAS TAMALE SAUSAGE

Making sausage from scratch is a daunting task, even for the most experienced pitmaster. I even doubted whether to include this recipe in the book, but it's one of the most successful sausages I've made, debuting in 2020. As a kid growing up in a Hispanic household, one of the most consistent dishes we ate every year was tamales during Christmas. It was like a family reunion during the holidays, as my uncles, aunts, and cousins would all gather at my grandparents' house to make hundreds of pounds of corn masa and make over 1,200 tamales every year. We'd eat them until we were sick, then freeze the rest and eat them over the following months, or give them away to friends. This sausage brings back those flavors and memories sealed inside of a smoky pork casing.

Perhaps one of our most popular handcrafted sausages, it requires multiple days of preparation to achieve the right texture and level of flavor a great tamale is known for. If you don't get it right the first time (or third), keep experimenting and do what works best for you.

### FOR TAMALE SAUSAGE SLURRY

1½ cups (180 g) dark chili powder
⅓ cup (53 g) kosher salt
⅓ cup (32 g) ground black pepper
¼ cup (40 g) granulated garlic
¼ cup (28 g) ground cumin
2 tablespoons (10 g) cayenne pepper
1 tablespoon (19 g) pink curing salt
4 cups (480 g) ice cubes

### FOR PORK

9 pounds (4 kg) boneless pork shoulder, cut into 1½-inch (3.5 cm) cubes
1 cup (125 g) dry milk powder

### FOR GUAJILLO BRAISED PORK SHOULDER

6 pounds (2.7 kg) boneless pork shoulder, cut into 1½-inch (3.5 cm) cubes
½ cup (60 g) dark chili powder
¼ cup (40 g) kosher salt
2 tablespoons (6 g) dried Mexican oregano

5 dried guajillo chiles
5 cups (1.2 L) water
½ white onion
5 garlic cloves, peeled
1 bay leaf

1 pound (454 g) cooked tamale masa (according to the package directions)
Whole hog casings (35 to 38 mm; enough for 20 pounds, or 9 kg)

**CONTINUED** ➤➤

1. To prepare the tamale sausage slurry, in a blender, combine the slurry ingredients and pulse for 12 to 15 seconds until you have a "smoothie" texture.

2. To prepare the pork, in a very large bowl or food-safe container, combine the 9 pounds (4 kg) of pork cubes and the slurry. Refrigerate covered in plastic wrap overnight.

3. Feed the pork into a meat grinder through a ½-inch (1 cm) plate. Refrigerate the ground pork for 15 to 20 minutes.

4. Place a ¼-inch (0.6 cm) plate on the grinder and feed the pork through it. Mix in the milk powder until well combined. Refrigerate the ground pork covered in plastic wrap.

5. Preheat a smoker to 275°F (140°C).

6. To prepare the guajillo braised pork shoulder, season the 6 pounds (2.7 kg) of cubed pork with chili powder, salt, and oregano. Place the pork in the smoker for 1 to 2 hours.

7. While the pork cooks, in a pot over medium heat, combine the guajillo chiles with enough water to cover. Cook for 5 to 7 minutes to soften. Drain the chiles, stem them, and place in a blender with 5 cups (1.2 L) water. Purée until smooth. Strain the chiles through a fine-mesh sieve into a bowl.

8. Transfer the braised pork chunks from the smoker to a half hotel (12 × 10-inch, or 30 × 25 cm) pan. Add the strained guajillo purée, white onion, garlic, and bay leaf. Wrap the pan tightly with aluminum foil and return the pork

to the smoker. Cook for 1 to 2 hours longer, or until the pork is fork tender. Remove from the heat, remove the bay leaf, shred the meat with two forks, and refrigerate covered in plastic wrap overnight.

9. To stuff and cook the sausage, in a large food-safe container (I use a large bus tub), combine the raw ground pork, guajillo braised pork, and cooked tamale masa. Mix by hand or with a meat mixer for 8 to 10 minutes until well combined. Add water if necessary to create "tackiness" and ensure the sausage mixture isn't dry.

**CONTINUED** ➤➤

10. Load the sausage mixture into the sausage stuffer hopper two to three handfuls at a time, pressing down firmly each time to prevent air pockets in the hopper.

11. Once the hopper is full, rinse the casings 2 to 3 times and then soak them in warm water for 15 to 20 minutes.

12. Thread the casings onto the horn and stuff them slowly, ensuring the casings stay wet and do not break. Make a coil with the stuffed sausage, then link one roughly 4½ inches (11 cm) in length by pinching the link at both ends and twisting it. It should weigh roughly 5.3 ounces (151 g). Use this link as a template for how long each sausage should be and twist the remaining links. Carefully cut apart the links and set them on a wire rack, then refrigerate overnight. Do not cover—they need to air dry to help the casings "snap" once cooked.

13. Once the sausages have chilled overnight, start a bundle fire in a smoker with a small bed of coals and wood chunks or a small split of pecan or post oak wood on top. The temperature should be between 120°F and 130°F (49°C and 54°C).

14. Place the links in the smoker and focus on maintaining proper temperature—making sure not to get too hot, but create lots of smoke to "cold smoke" your sausages. Cook for 3½ to 4 hours. The sausages should have a deep red color and register an internal temperature between 145°F and 150°F (63°C and 65.5°C).

15. Just before removing the sausages, prepare an ice bath.

16. Transfer the sausages from the smoker to the ice bath for 1 to 2 minutes. Remove the sausages from the ice bath, dry them, and store in a vacuum-sealed bag or zip-top bag until ready to heat for serving. When reheating, smoke at 250°F (120°C) or heat in a 300°F (149°C) oven for 25 to 30 minutes until they reach 140°F (60°C). Serve immediately.

# BEEF RIB CHILI

Chili is one of those dishes that everyone makes, but not everyone makes it with a smoked beef rib that would typically cost $50 to $65 at a craft barbecue restaurant. When I operated out of a food trailer, I'd sometimes have trouble selling out of beef ribs and would be left with two or three racks that I couldn't reheat to sell again. So, I figured, beef rib chili—why the hell not? It was an instant hit and I found myself selling more beef rib chili than I could smoke beef ribs to make. Compared to brisket chili or ground chuck chili, this chili is super rich thanks to the marbling in the beef ribs. I like to leave the bones in the chili so any marrow adds extra flavor (and for a super-cool aesthetic).

2 tablespoons (30 ml) canola oil

1 white onion, diced

4 garlic cloves, minced

1 jalapeño pepper, minced

4 ounces (115 g) tomato paste

1 (28-ounce, or 794 g) can crushed San Marzano tomatoes

2 cups (480 ml) beef stock

12 ounces (360 ml) beer (such as Negro Modelo)

2 pounds (908 g) smoked beef ribs (see page 104), cut into 1-inch (2.5 cm) cubes

¼ cup (30 g) dark chili powder

2 tablespoons (20 g) kosher salt

2 tablespoons (20 g) granulated garlic

1 tablespoon (7 g) ground white pepper

1 tablespoon (6 g) ground black pepper

1 tablespoon (7 g) paprika

1 teaspoon ground cumin

1 teaspoon dried Mexican oregano

Shredded cheddar cheese, for garnish

Minced red onion, for garnish

Sliced jalapeño peppers, for garnish

1. Preheat a smoker to 250°F (120°C) using post oak wood.

2. In a stockpot over medium heat, heat the oil until hot. Add the onion, garlic, and jalapeño. Sauté for 2 to 3 minutes, stirring constantly. Stir in the tomato paste until incorporated.

3. Pour in the crushed tomatoes, stock, and beer, and stir well.

4. Add the beef ribs and all the spices. Stir well to ensure the ingredients are incorporated. Transfer the pot to the smoker. Cook for 4 hours until thickened. The beef ribs are already cooked. Time in the smoker will help the flavors meld and impart smoke flavor into the chili from the post oak.

5. Serve with shredded cheddar and minced red onion to garnish. Add sliced jalapeños for a kick.

# PULLED PORK CARNITAS

Remember when I said how versatile pork shoulder is? This is one of those recipes that takes a little bit of effort to prep, but will transport you to Michoacán when you take your first smoky bite of a taco packed with chopped carnitas, and a little bit of savory pork fat drips down your lip.

1 tablespoon (10 g) kosher salt

1 tablespoon (8.5 g) restaurant-style ground black pepper

1 tablespoon (7.5 g) dark chili powder

1 teaspoon smoked paprika

1 teaspoon granulated garlic

1 teaspoon ground cumin

1 teaspoon dried Mexican oregano

3 to 4 pounds (1.3 to 18 kg) boneless pork shoulder, cut into 2½- to 3-inch (6 to 7.5 cm) chunks

1 white onion, diced

4 garlic cloves, minced

2 cups (480 ml) cola (preferably Mexican Coke)

1 cup (240 ml) fresh orange juice

1 cup (240 ml) chicken stock

1 cup (206 g) beef tallow or pork lard

Grated zest of 1 orange

Pico de Gallo (page 149) or store-bought, for serving

4.5-inch (11 cm)-corn tortillas, for serving

1. Preheat a smoker to 250°F (120°C) using pecan or post oak wood.

2. In a small bowl, stir together the spices and season the pork shoulder with them liberally on all sides. Place the pork in the smoker, spreading the chunks so they do not touch or crowd each other. Smoke for 3 to 4 hours, or until the pork begins to take on a mahogany color. Remove the pork from the smoker.

3. In a 9 × 13-inch (23 × 33 cm) baking dish, combine the onion and garlic. Place the pork on top. Pour the cola, orange juice, stock, and beef tallow over the pork and sprinkle with the orange zest. Cover the pan tightly with aluminum foil and place it in the smoker at 300°F (150°C) for 2 to 3 hours longer, or until the pork reaches an internal temperature between 185°F and 190°F (85°C and 88°C) and is tender. Remove the carnitas from the smoker.

4. Preheat the oven to 450°F (230°C, or gas mark 8). With a fork or wooden spatula, lightly "shred" the carnitas in the pan. Roast for 10 to 12 minutes, or until the pork begins to crisp and brown on top.

5. Garnish with pico de gallo and serve immediately in a taco.

# BARBECUE PLATTERS: PRACTICAL PLATING

**THE PHONE EATS FIRST.**

There's an age-old adage that people eat first with their eyes, meaning that the presentation of a plate, or tray of barbecue, is almost more important than how it tastes. That would be true if not for the sudden influx of content creators, Yelp elitists, and "foodie" ambassadors across the world who share content on social media with their mobile phone-fueled restaurant reviews where, undoubtedly, the phone eats first. Admittedly, my food trailer started with barbecue platters that were disorganized and had little rhyme or reason to the way they were plated.

Over time, I discovered that although "pretty" trays looked great, practicality made more of an impact on the overall customer experience, and the product I was serving looked better when transferred from the pit to their platter.

If visiting a historic barbecue restaurant like Kreuz Market or Smitty's Market in Lockhart, Texas, you could expect your meats to be served on peach butcher paper the same way they've done it for over a century. The same could be said for modern-day craft barbecue restaurants like Goldee's BBQ (*Texas Monthly*'s number-one barbecue joint in 2021) in Fort Worth, Texas. Co-owner Lane Milne says, "What makes Goldee's plating stand out, I think, are the warm, earthy tones and how the colors interact with other ones in our dining space. We strive to build a variety of heights and a variety of 'flows' in the way the meats, sides, desserts, and pickles interact on the tray. We also use other meats to protect the brisket from oxidation. When we have a long line of people waiting, we make sure our cutting and portioning is efficient and concise."

Plating for practicality can be broken down into six functional steps, which yield a better result when it comes time to eat. After all, if you've spent hours upon hours tending a fire until you smell like a pit room yourself, you want to make sure your precious proteins are plated in a way you can be proud of while cooking for family or friends.

CONTINUED ▶▶

1. **Butcher paper as a base.** Butcher paper (no matter the color) helps absorb the grease from brisket, ribs, sausage, and other fatty proteins. I recommend starting with a metal tray first, then layering one or two sheets of butcher paper on it. It's also a cool aesthetic that helps give your party an official "Texas barbecue" vibe.

2. **Set your sides down first.** Side dishes tend to stay hot longer and hold better if they're in foam cups or paper boats. I usually recommend plating them first and building your proteins around them. You can keep them all together on one side of the tray or spread them out to serve as boundaries to contain your proteins within.

3. **Plate your proteins quickly.** Oxygen is the number-one enemy of sliced meats. From the second you slice into a brisket or rack of pork ribs, a timer begins until your proteins begin to oxidize and turn an ugly, cold gray color that is unappealing. The order in which you slice your proteins is also important and can help prevent oxidization on your platter. If you've cut into your meats but need more time to plate them correctly, wrapping them in plastic wrap will prevent them from oxidizing quickly while you continue to construct your tray.

CONTINUED ▶▶

4. **Layer your meats.** Layering your proteins on the platter not only prevents them from oxidizing faster, but it helps insulate the meats and can keep them warm longer rather than slicing and serving them all separately. I generally start with sliced brisket on the bottom and like to lay fattier slices from the point on the lean slices from the flat, which have less marbling and tend to dry out more quickly. From there, the plate is my canvas. If using an array of meats, I slice turkey breast next and lay those slices up against the brisket to act as a cradle for pork ribs, which typically go on top. Pork ribs tend to show the least amount of oxidization because they're sauced or glazed, so I usually angle them over the brisket and turkey breast to keep those meats warm. Then, I utilize the natural curvature of sausages around pulled pork that's balled up to keep those meats close together and warm longer.

5. **Tacos and accoutrements.** Once my sides and proteins are plated, if adding street tacos or birria, I look for gaps in the tray where butcher paper is still peeking through and fill those gaps with tacos for the ultimate Tex-Mex barbecue tray. And the typical Texas barbecue platter is always accompanied by dill pickles (preferably homemade) and pickled red onions, which you can place on the corners of your platter, or in other areas where butcher paper still shows.

6. **Soak it all up.** When I first started the food trailer, and for the first three years of our brick and mortar, I didn't serve bread with any of our barbecue. That may seem sacrilegious, but I've never fit within the confines of traditional barbecue and have always served fresh flour tortillas in lieu of white bread. Since I started catering more over the last two years, customers constantly request white bread, so it's available now upon request, but I always suggest warm flour tortillas first. There's just something about a fatty brisket taco that you can't quite get from a white bread foldover. If serving tortillas with your barbecue, fold three or four in half, then in half again to make sort of a pocket square you can tuck away in your tray of goodness for people to indulge in.

# TACOS Y MAS

# TACOS ARE THE VESSELS

that connect Texans to Mexican heritage through food. They're a blank canvas for creativity, and can be complex, sophisticated recipes that require hours of preparation, or they can be overly simple with wholesome ingredients that speak for themselves. I've done both, and I keep a rotating taco special on the menu to keep things interesting at my restaurants—aside from the staples people expect, such as brisket birria tacos.

# MILANESA TACOS

This taco is anything but traditional, but if you can imagine a Tex-Mex chicken-fried steak taco with an earthy, garlicky hot sauce, that's exactly what it is. Milanesa is typically served by itself or inside of a torta, but I much prefer it in a flour tortilla. The green chile gravy adds a kick, but the real sleeper is the chile de árbol sauce. It's earthy, spicy, nutty, and garlicky all at once.

## FOR CHILE DE ÁRBOL SAUCE

8 to 10 dried chiles de árbol
4 dried guajillo chiles
4 garlic cloves, peeled
2 Roma tomatoes
¾ cup (180 ml) reserved
   soaking water
1 teaspoon kosher salt
½ teaspoon ground cumin
1 cup (240 ml) canola oil

## FOR GREEN CHILE GRAVY

4 tablespoons (½ stick, or 56 g)
   unsalted butter
2 tablespoons (30 g) canned
   diced green chiles
2 tablespoons (15.5 g) all-
   purpose flour
2 cups (480 ml) heavy
   whipping cream
1 teaspoon kosher salt, plus
   more as needed
1 teaspoon ground black pepper
1 teaspoon granulated garlic
½ teaspoon ground cumin

## FOR TACOS

Canola oil, for frying
2 cups (240 g) biscuit mix
1 teaspoon kosher salt, plus more
   as needed
1 teaspoon ground black pepper
1 teaspoon granulated garlic
1 teaspoon smoked paprika
½ teaspoon cayenne pepper
1 large egg
½ cup (120 ml) milk
1 teaspoon hot sauce (such as
   Valentina)
1 pound (454 g) Tex-Mex Smoked
   Brisket (page 89), or store-
   bought, chilled and cut into
   ¼-inch (0.6 cm) thick slices
4 (6-inch, or 15 cm) flour tortillas,
   warmed
Chopped fresh cilantro, for
   garnish

1. To prepare the chile de árbol sauce, in a sauce-pan, combine the chiles de árbol, guajillo chiles, garlic, tomatoes, and enough water to cover. Bring to a boil over high heat and continue to boil for 15 to 20 seconds. Remove the pot from the heat and cover with a lid. Let stand for 10 minutes so the chiles "steep." With a slotted spoon, transfer the chiles, garlic, and tomatoes to a blender. Add the ¾ cup (180 ml) reserved soaking water, salt, and cumin. Blend for 8 to 10 seconds until smooth. Strain the sauce through a fine-mesh sieve into a bowl and return it to the blender. Turn the blender on low speed and slowly add the canola oil to thicken the sauce. It should begin to turn a vibrant orange color as you add the oil. Set aside.

2. To prepare the green chile gravy, in a clean saucepan or cast-iron skillet over medium-high heat, melt the butter. Add the green chiles and sauté for 2 to 3 minutes. Add the flour and cook for 3 to 4 minutes, stirring constantly, until the flour is a light brown color. While stirring constantly, slowly pour in the heavy cream, making sure the flour is completely cooked without lumps. Add the spices and cook for 2 to 3 minutes, stirring, or until the gravy thickens. Taste and add more salt as needed.

3. To prepare the tacos, in a cast-iron skillet over medium-high heat, heat 2 to 3 inches (5 to 7.5 cm) of oil to 350°F (180°C).

4. Build a dredge station: In a medium-size shallow bowl, whisk the biscuit mix, salt, black pepper, granulated garlic, smoked paprika, and cayenne. In a second shallow bowl, whisk the egg, milk, and hot sauce until smooth. Dredge the chilled sliced brisket in the biscuit mix, then the egg wash, and back into the biscuit mix until evenly coated all over. Carefully place the brisket slices in the hot oil and fry for 2 to 3 minutes per side until golden brown. Season to taste with salt and place on a wire rack to cool.

5. To assemble the tacos, place the fried brisket inside a warm flour tortilla. Ladle the green chile gravy over the brisket, then drizzle the chile de árbol sauce across the taco. Garnish with cilantro and serve immediately.

# BEST WOODS
## FOR SMOKING

Wood is a crucial part of smoking, but don't stress too much. The only real rule is to pick a hardwood (deciduous trees) because softwoods (evergreens) have a higher moisture content and sap, so they burn quickly with black, acrid smoke. Hardwood is dense, smolders slowly, and produces a clean, white smoke, which is perfect for infusing flavor.

Certain types of wood are used in Tex-Mex barbecue, and specific ones are referenced in my recipes. Regarding Texas, the commonly used woods regionally are hickory in the east/north of Texas, post oak in central Texas, and mesquite in the south/west. Fruit, pecan, and other nut wood are found throughout the state.

**HICKORY:** This is one of the most used woods because of availability and its unique flavor profile. The strong smoke is sweetish and adds deep color, but it can get bitter if you don't burn a clean fire. Hickory is suitable for large cuts of meat and long cooks.

**POST OAK:** This wood produces a mild, pleasing smoky flavor that allows the natural taste of the food to shine through. It is perfect for longer cooks because of its consistent heat and lower burn temperature. Oak adds a mild smoke flavor to meat and is excellent for building bark on cuts like brisket. Post oak is most commonly used in central Texas and is the preferred wood at most Texas barbecue joints.

**MESQUITE:** This wood burns hot and fast and generates lots of smoke, producing an intense flavor that can become bitter if the meat is smoked too long. Mesquite is most commonly used for grilling proteins. There's nothing quite like the taste of mesquite-grilled beef fajitas.

**PECAN:** Pecan produces a moderate, sweet, nutty flavor and it's often mixed with other woods to balance their strong, distinctive taste. Some barbecue joints prefer to mix pecan with oak when smoking meats, because of how well they complement each other. Pecan burns faster and hotter than oak, though, so it's important to maintain proper fire management if using pecan.

# PASTRAMI TACOS

Pastrami takes patience, especially when brining an entire brisket for six to seven days just to spend twelve hours tending a fire to smoke it. I don't always have a week to prepare a menu item, which is why I use tri-tip for this dish. It takes way less time to brine, and cooks significantly faster, yielding a tastier taco in only a few days. The pickled mustard seed can be prepared while you're waiting on your tri-tip to brine, as it takes a couple of days for the flavors to meld. This taco is nontraditional at best, but tastes like a visit to Katz's Deli in New York, folded inside of a warm corn tortilla.

## FOR TRI-TIP

1 gallon (3.8 L) water
¾ cup (120 g) kosher salt
½ cup (100 g) granulated sugar
2 tablespoons (12.5 g) pickling spice
1 tablespoon (8.5 g) whole black peppercorns
1 tablespoon (5 g) coriander seeds
2 teaspoons pink curing salt
4 garlic cloves, peeled
2 whole tri-tips (2 to 3 pounds, or 908 g to 1.3 kg, each)
Ground black pepper
10 (6-inch, or 15 cm) corn tortillas (blue corn masa if possible)

## FOR PICKLED MUSTARD SEEDS

1 cup (176 g) yellow mustard seeds
1 cup (240 ml) white vinegar
2 garlic cloves, peeled
½ cup (120 ml) water
½ cup (100 g) granulated sugar
1 teaspoon kosher salt
½ teaspoon red chili flakes

## FOR SLAW

1 cup (240 g) mayonnaise
¼ cup (60 ml) apple cider vinegar
¼ cup (50 g) granulated sugar
¼ cup (80 g) honey
1 teaspoon kosher salt
1 teaspoon ground black pepper
1 teaspoon red chili flakes
½ teaspoon granulated garlic
4 cups (170 g) shredded green cabbage
½ cup (46 g) julienned red bell pepper
½ cup (53 g) julienned red onion

**CONTINUED ▶▶**

1. To prepare the tri-tip, pour the water into a large pot over medium-high heat. Add the kosher salt, sugar, pickling spice, peppercorns, coriander seeds, curing salt, and garlic and bring to a boil. Once the brine boils, turn off the heat and let cool to room temperature.

2. Place the tri-tips in a brining bucket or clean large pot and cover with the cooled brine. Set a heavy plate on top to keep the tri-tips submerged. Cover and refrigerate for 3 days.

3. To prepare the pickled mustard seeds, in a medium-size saucepan over medium-high heat, combine all the ingredients and bring to a boil. Turn the heat to low and simmer for 10 to 12 minutes. Remove from the heat. Transfer the mustard seeds and cooking liquid to a Mason jar and let cool. Cover the jar and refrigerate for at least 24 hours so the flavors intensify.

4. To cook the pastrami, preheat a smoker to 250°F (120°C) using post oak or pecan wood.

5. Remove the tri-tips from the brine, pat dry, and season with pepper (the brine has enough salt and any more would be overpowering). Place the tri-tips in the smoker and smoke for 4 to 5 hours, or until the tri-tips reach an internal temperature between 195°F and 203°F (90.5°C and 95°C). Remove and let rest, tented with foil.

6. To prepare the slaw, in a large bowl, whisk the mayo, vinegar, sugar, honey, salt, black pepper, red chili flakes, and granulated garlic until smooth and combined. Add the cabbage, bell pepper, and onion. Toss to combine.

7. To assemble the tacos, toast the tortillas on a plancha or an open flame for 10 to 12 seconds per side to char. Slice the smoked tri-tip against the grain in ¼-inch (0.6 cm)-thick slices and layer 2 or 3 slices on each tortilla. Spoon the slaw on the taco and finish with a teaspoon of pickled mustard seeds. Serve immediately.

# BARBECUE
## *PORTION SIZES*

There's no exact answer to the amount of cooked meat you'll need for each person, but generally, you can plan for:

- **BRISKET:** ½ to 1 pound (225 to 455 g) per person

- **PULLED PORK:** ⅓ to ½ pound (151 to 225 g) per person (served on a bun reduces the amount to ¼ pound [115 g])

- **RIBS:** 3–4 ribs per person (baby back pork ribs); 2–3 ribs per person (pork spareribs); 3–4 ribs per person (St. Louis–style ribs)

- **STEAK:** ½ to ¾ pound (225 to 340 g) per person

Factors that influence the amount of meat needed include:

**MULTIPLE TYPES OF MEAT:** Generally speaking, most adults will eat a total of ⅓ to ½ pound (151 to 225g) of meat, and children will eat about ¼ pound (115 g) of meat.

**THE TYPE OF GET-TOGETHER:** Tailgates or backyard get-togethers will require more food than a more formal sit down event.

**SIDE DISHES OR DESSERTS:** Other food choices will fill up your guests and they will often save room for something sweet at the end of the meal. The type of sides will also influence meat portions. Light salads are less filling than potato salad or mac and cheese.

**TIME OF DAY:** People eat more at dinner time than at lunch.

**DURATION:** The longer the event, the more people will eat—even returning for seconds later.

**ALCOHOL:** When guests drink alcohol, they usually eat more food.

# MEXICAN CORN BREAD MUFFINS

This ain't ya' Mama's average corn bread, but it's a version of my mama's Mexican corn bread that I grew up eating. Hers was made in a skillet with ground beef and could be considered a meal in itself. My version is served with smoky chopped brisket topped with honey butter for a sweet and savory finish.

4 cups (624) corn bread mix

1 teaspoon baking powder

1 teaspoon granulated sugar

1 teaspoon kosher salt

1 cup (240 ml) water

¼ cup (60 ml) canola oil

6 tablespoons (84 g) unsalted butter, melted, plus more butter for serving

½ cup (60 g) shredded cheddar cheese

½ cup (83 g) frozen corn kernels

¼ cup (38 g) diced jalapeño pepper

¼ cup (40 g) diced white onion

¼ cup (4 g) chopped fresh cilantro

6 ounces (170 g) chopped Tex-Mex Smoked Brisket (page 89), or store-bought

Honey, for serving

1. Preheat the oven to 375°F (190°C, or gas mark 5). Spray a muffin tin heavily with nonstick cooking spray.

2. In a large bowl, whisk the corn bread mix, baking powder, sugar, and salt to combine well. Add the water, oil, and melted butter. Whisk until smooth.

3. Add the cheese, vegetables, cilantro, and brisket to the batter and fold it in with a spatula. Fill each prepared muffin cup with ¼ cup (28 g) of batter.

4. Bake for 12 to 14 minutes, or until the muffins are cooked through and a toothpick inserted into the middle comes out clean.

5. Serves the muffins topped with a dollop of butter and a drizzle of honey.

# BRISKET BIRRIA TACOS

Birria tacos are the number-one most popular item at my restaurants, and this recipe is sure to become one of your favorite dishes at home. One of the best things about this birria meat is you can vacuum-seal it and freeze it, and the consommé, for later if you don't eat it all in one sitting. The most important aspect of this dish is smoking the brisket first. It creates a whole new level of flavor in the tacos, and is a great way to use brisket trim if you're tired of burgers and sausage. Don't skim the fat from the consommé like some recipes call for. It's necessary to dip and fry the tortillas in, creating that deep red color that good birria tacos are known for.

### FOR BRISKET
**10 pounds (4.5 kg) brisket trim**
**12 ounces (340 g) Hurtado Beef Blend (page 28)**

### FOR CONSOMMÉ
**1½ gallons (5.8 L) water**
**5 dried guajillo chiles, stemmed**
**½ cup (15 g) dried chiles de árbol, stemmed**
**5 Roma tomatoes**
**½ white onion**
**6 garlic cloves, peeled**
**2 tablespoons (40 g) beef base**
**2 tablespoons (20 g) kosher salt**
**1 tablespoon (10 g) granulated garlic**
**1 tablespoon (7 g) onion powder**
**1 teaspoon ground cumin**
**1 teaspoon dried Mexican oregano**
**1 cinnamon stick**
**2 tablespoons (17 g) whole peppercorns**
**1 tablespoon (12 g) star anise pods**

### FOR ASSEMBLY
**12 (6-inch, or 15 cm) corn tortillas**
**1 pound (454 g) quesadilla cheese or mozzarella, shredded**
**12 ounces (340 g) Smoked Salsa Verde (page 43)**
**1 cup (16 g) fresh cilantro, chopped**
**1 cup (160 g) chopped white onion**

1. Preheat a smoker to 250°F (120°C).

2. To prepare the brisket, season the brisket trim on all sides with the beef blend. Place the brisket in the smoker and cook for 4½ to 5 hours, or until the bark is beginning to set.

3. To prepare the consommé, while the meat smokes, in a large pot, combine the water, dried chiles, tomatoes, onion, garlic, beef base, salt, granulated garlic, onion powder, cumin, and oregano. In a cheesecloth square, combine the cinnamon, peppercorns, and star anise. Tie the sachet to hold the spices and drop it into the pot. Set aside the consommé until the brisket is ready to add.

4. To finish the brisket, once the internal temperature is 165°F (74°C), remove it from the smoker and add it to the consommé. Cook over medium-low heat for 3 to 3½ hours, or until the meat probes like butter and falls apart. Remove the meat from the broth. Remove and discard the cheesecloth sachet. Strain the consommé through a fine-mesh sieve into a bowl and return it to the pot. Transfer the solids (chiles, tomatoes, onion, garlic) in the sieve to a blender. Add 3 cups (720 ml) of the consommé and blend for 7 to 8 seconds on high speed until smooth. Pour the blended solids into the consommé. Put the pot over medium heat and simmer the consommé so the fat rises to the top.

5. To build the tacos, one at a time, dip the tortillas into the consommé and place on a well-seasoned plancha over medium-high heat. Cook for 10 to 12 seconds until the tortillas start to bubble. Flip the tortillas and spread a handful of cheese over each. Place 2 tablespoons (28 g) of the birria meat on one side of each tortilla. Drizzle the salsa verde over each taco and sprinkle about 1 tablespoon (1 g) of the cilantro and some onion over each. Fold the tacos over (meat-side on top) so gravity holds the taco closed and adheres to the melted cheese. Cook the tacos on the plancha for 1 to 2 minutes, or until the bottoms are crispy. They should have a deep red color, but ladle some of the birria fat skimmed from the top of the consommé over them to add color if needed. Flip the tacos and cook for 1 to 2 minutes more.

6. Serve immediately, garnished with cilantro and onion.

# BRISKET "BARBACOA" TACOS

This taco is one of the best ways to repurpose brisket trim other than using it for sausage or hamburger grind. The "mohawk" is typically cut off the top of the brisket point to make the meat aerodynamic (see how to trim a brisket, page 89) This chunk of meat is rich, fatty, and full of flavor, making it perfect to cook barbacoa with. Cooked nearly exactly like a brisket, you'll have a hard time telling the difference between beef cheek, or "cachet," and this piece of brisket trim.

To cut the meat, grab the mohawk from the top of the brisket point and "pinch" it to expose it from the rest of the meat. Slice it from the flat toward the back of the point, leaving you with a 1- to 1½-pound (454 to 681 g) hunk of fatty meat, or a "mini brisket."

---

⅓ cup (32 g) ground black pepper

2 tablespoons (20 g) kosher salt

1 teaspoon granulated garlic

1 teaspoon seasoned salt

1 teaspoon chili powder

½ teaspoon ground cumin

2 brisket "mohawks," trimmed
    off the point

¼ cup (44 g) yellow mustard

½ cup (58 g) julienned white
    onion

4 cups (960 ml) beef stock

8 (4-inch, or 10 cm) mini corn
    tortillas

1 cup (128 g) Smoked Salsa
    Verde (page 43)

1 cup (16 g) chopped fresh
    cilantro

1 cup (160 g) chopped white
    onion

1. Preheat a smoker to 250°F (120°C) using post oak or pecan wood.

2. In a small bowl, stir together the pepper, kosher salt, granulated garlic, seasoned salt, chili powder, and cumin. Rub the yellow mustard all over the mohawks to help the rub adhere and liberally season both mohawks all over with the spice mix. Place the mohawks in the smoker and manage the fire for 4 to 5 hours to remain between 225°F and 250°F (107°C and 120°C). Once the mohawks reach an internal temperature between 180°F and 185°F (82°C and 85°C), place the julienned onion in a half-size aluminum foil pan and place the brisket on the onion.

3. Pour the stock over the mohawks, then wrap the pan tightly in foil and place it back in the smoker. Continue to cook at 250°F (120°C) for 1 to 2 hours longer, or until the meat probes 205°F to 208°F (96°C to 98°C). It may take a little longer to fully render the fat.

4. Remove the meat from the pan and save the au jus and onion.

5. Chop the mohawks or massage them by hand until they shred and fall apart, adding the au jus to help keep the meat moist.

6. Toast the tortillas over a plancha for 10 seconds per side, then add some meat to each taco. Drizzle salsa verde over the tacos and garnish with cilantro and chopped onion.

# HOW TO WRAP A
# BRISKET

Aluminum foil is a traditional material for wrapping meat. Foil is easy to handle, and most people have it in their kitchen. Foil creates a tight seal that traps heat, speeds up cooking time, and does not allow further smoke to infuse the meat. The meat's juices are reabsorbed when removed from the smoker, but this trapped moisture also creates a softer, less crunchy bark. The main thing for me if using foil is to ensure the bark has set so it doesn't wash off when you wrap the meat. That's usually around 180°F to 185°F (82°C to 85°C) internal temperature.

Butcher paper is popular with Texas-style barbecue. It is slightly porous, so smoke can seep in, adding flavor, and moisture can leak out, maintaining the crunchy bark. Butcher paper does not affect cooking time.

The wrapping method I prefer is called a burrito wrap or Texas crutch.

Place overlapping sheets (three times longer than your meat is wide) of butcher paper or foil on a work surface, with a long edge perpendicular to you. Place the meat lengthwise on the wrap about one foot from the bottom, with the curved side facing you. Fold the bottom edge of the paper over the top of the meat on the curved side as tight as possible. Pinch the paper, hold it down with one hand, and fold the other side end over the point and flat of the meat so it is even over each end and there are no gaps. Then fold the paper over again, fold the ends over, and pull the brisket to you tightly to ensure there are no air pockets. Continue folding until the paper is all wrapped up.

# TEXAS "TWINKIES"

The Texas Twinkie was first invented by Hutchins Barbeque in McKinney, Texas, but has since been replicated and recreated by dozens of barbecue restaurants across the state over the last ten years. My version is similar to the famous Hutchins Twinkie with two exceptions: I use a homemade pimiento cheese filling in lieu of cream cheese, and I smoke the Twinkies all the way through as opposed to grilling them. I will say this: Hutchins has the best Texas Twinkies in the state, but these are a close second.

12 extra-large jalapeño peppers
1 pound (454 g) pimiento cheese
1 pound (454 g) chopped
   Tex-Mex Smoked Brisket
   (page 89), or store-bought
24 bacon slices (about 2 pounds,
   or 908 g)
2 tablespoons (20 g) kosher salt
⅓ cup (32 g) ground black pepper
2 cups (480 ml) My Sweet Sauce
   (page 33)
Chopped fresh cilantro, for
   garnish

1. Preheat a smoker to 250°F (120°C).

2. Halve the jalapeños lengthwise and remove the seeds and veins with a spoon. Leave the stems. Fill the peppers on one side with 1½ ounces (43 g) of the pimiento cheese and the other side with 1½ ounces (43 g) of the chopped brisket. Close the two halves and wrap the jalapeño tightly with about 4 bacon slices. Season with salt and pepper.

3. Place the filled peppers in the smoker and cook for 1½ hours, or until the bacon is cooked through and the peppers have a mahogany color.

4. Glaze the peppers with the sauce and let them smoke for 10 to 12 minutes longer until they're mahogany in color and the bacon is crispy.

5. Remove from the smoker and garnish with cilantro and any remaining sauce.

# BIG RED BARBACOA TOSTADAS

This tostada is what my restaurant was most known for during COVID, a time when brisket was unavailable and supply chains across the globe were completely disrupted. Because it was so difficult to find brisket, which is the number-one protein of any Texas barbecue joint, we had to pivot to remain open and find other beef products, such as cheek meat, tri-tip, and shoulder clod. By and large, this tostada is one of the best things I've ever eaten in Texas barbecue. The Big Red soda adds a depth of sweet and savory flavor that is unmatched in any beef cheek dish I've ever had. The texture from the homemade tostada shell makes every bite an adventure in your mouth. Don't buy pre-made tostada shells—it's well worth doing it from scratch.

1 cup (240 ml) vegetable oil

4 (6-inch or 15 cm) corn tortillas

2 cups (512 g) refried beans

1 pound (454 g) Big Red Barbacoa (page 98)

4 tablespoons (4 g) chopped fresh cilantro

4 tablespoons (40 g) chopped white onion

½ cup (64 g) Smoked Salsa Verde (page 43)

4 tablespoons (20 g) shredded Cotija cheese

Hot sauce (such as Valentina), for serving

1. In a large skillet over medium-high heat, heat the oil until hot. Carefully add the tortillas and fry for 2 to 3 minutes, then flip them and cook for 2 to 3 minutes longer, or until crispy. Transfer to a wire rack.

2. To build the tostadas, spread 4 tablespoons (64 g) of the refried beans over each tostada shell. Top each with 4 ounces (115 g) of the barbacoa.

3. Sprinkle 1 tablespoon (1 g) of the cilantro and 1 tablespoon (10 g) of the onion over each tostada.

4. Drizzle each with salsa verde, then spoon 1 tablespoon (5 g) of the Cotija cheese over each.

5. Finish by drizzling hot sauce across each tostada to serve.

# SMOKED TRI-TIP TACOS

This tri-tip taco combines the bold flavors of California grilled tri-tip with Central Texas–style smoke. This is one of those rare instances where it's okay to use mesquite wood for smoking and grilling. I don't like smoking with mesquite wood because it can be bitter, but I love grilling with mesquite wood at higher temperatures. I use a reverse sear method here to achieve the perfect sear and medium-rare temperature, making this a taco you won't soon forget.

## FOR TRI-TIP

**1 Prime grade tri-tip (2 to 3 pounds, or 908 g to 1.3 kg)**
**⅓ cup (about 75 g) Hurtado Beef Blend (page 28)**
**4 (6-inch, or 15 cm) flour tortillas**
**Cilantro Lime Crema (page 47), for garnish**
**Chopped fresh cilantro, for garnish**
**Lime wedges, for garnish**

## FOR PICO DE GALLO

**3 Roma tomatoes, diced**
**⅓ cup (53 g) diced red onion**
**¼ cup (4 g) fresh cilantro, chopped**
**¼ cup (60 ml) fresh lime juice**
**Grated zest of 1 lime**
**1 tablespoon (9 g) diced jalapeño pepper**
**1 teaspoon kosher salt**
**½ teaspoon garlic salt**
**½ teaspoon ground cumin**

1. Preheat a smoker to 225°F (107°C) so the tri-tip gets plenty of smoke in the beginning of the cook.

2. To prepare the tri-tip, season the meat on all sides with the beef blend, then place it in the smoker for 30 to 45 minutes, using a temperature probe in the thickest part of the tri-tip, until it reaches an internal temperature of 115°F (46°C). Remove it from the smoker to sear it.

3. While the tri-tip cooks, make the pico and crema.

4. To prepare the pico, in a medium-size bowl, combine all ingredients and stir with a rubber spatula.

5. To finish the trip-tip, increase the smoker temperature to 500°F (250°C) and sear the meat on each side for 1 minute, or until the internal temperature is 125°F (52°C).

6. Toast the tortillas on a plancha over low-medium heat for 10 to 15 seconds per side.

7. Cut the tri-tip against the grain into ¼-inch (0.6 cm) slices and lay down 2 or 3 slices per tortilla. Spoon some pico over each and drizzle with crema. Garnish with cilantro and a lime wedge.

# BIRRIA RAMEN

This birria ramen is perfect for a cold winter day when you want something spicy and hearty to warm you up. It's prepared a little differently than the Birria Brisket Tacos (page 140), which are smoked first, but the process is similar otherwise. The shredded cheese makes a sort of "creamy" broth along with the egg yolk. For an added bonus, soak the soft-boiled eggs in soy sauce before cutting them.

---

**2 pounds (908 g) brisket trim or beef chuck roast, cut into chunks**

**4 dried guajillo chiles, stemmed**

**2 dried ancho chiles, stemmed**

**½ white onion**

**4 garlic cloves, minced**

**1 tablespoon (10 g) kosher salt**

**1 tablespoon (6 g) ground black pepper**

**1 tablespoon (3 g) dried Mexican oregano**

**1 teaspoon ground cumin**

**1 teaspoon ground cinnamon**

**4 cups (906 ml) beef stock**

**4 (3-ounce, or 85 g) packages ramen noodles (discard the seasoning it comes with)**

**2 cups (230 g) shredded mozzarella cheese**

**Sliced radishes, for garnish**

**1 cup (100 g) chopped scallion, green parts**

**4 large eggs, soft-boiled**

**Lime wedges, for garnish**

1. In a large pot, combine the beef, dried chiles, onion, garlic, salt, pepper, oregano, cumin, cinnamon, and stock. Bring to a boil over medium-high heat. Reduce the heat to low, cover the pot, and simmer for about 3 hours, or until the beef is tender and shreds easily. Remove the cooked beef from the pot and shred it using two forks. Set aside.

2. In a blender or food processor, blend the remaining cooking liquid, chiles, onion, and garlic until smooth. Return the blended mixture to the pot and bring the liquid to a simmer over medium-high heat. Add the shredded beef and cook for 30 minutes to meld the flavors.

3. While the birria simmers, cook the ramen noodles according to the package directions. Drain and set aside. For the lime garnish, sear half a lime on a hot skillet for 1 to 2 minutes (or an open flame on a hot grill for best results).

4. To serve, divide the cooked ramen noodles among four bowls. Place a handful of cheese over the noodles. Ladle the birria broth over the noodles to melt the cheese. Top each bowl with shredded beef, radishes, and scallion.

5. Serve the birria ramen with a soft-boiled egg on top and lime wedges on the side for squeezing.

# GUISADO DE RES

Guisado de res is the perfect meal to have for breakfast if you have leftover steaks from the night before. I've made this countless times at our family ranch with leftover steaks grilled on mesquite wood, which adds a ton of flavor. If using bone-in steaks, I like to leave the bone in for added depth and a cool aesthetic. Serve over flour tortillas to mop up all the gravy at the end of your meal.

4 **Roma tomatoes**

2 **dried guajillo chiles, stemmed and seeded**

1 **jalapeño pepper, stemmed**

4 **garlic cloves, peeled**

1 **white onion, halved**

1 **cup (240 ml) reserved cooking water**

1 **tablespoon (10 g) kosher salt, plus more as needed**

1 **teaspoon ground black pepper, plus more as needed**

1 **teaspoon granulated garlic**

1 **teaspoon dark chili powder**

½ **teaspoon ground cumin**

3 to 4 **tablespoons (45 to 60 ml) canola oil**

2 **pounds (908 g) steak, cubed (ribeye or strip steaks work best)**

1 **tablespoon (8 g) all-purpose flour**

8 **(6-inch, or 15 cm) flour tortillas**

1 **cup (16 g) chopped fresh cilantro**

1 **cup (160 g) chopped white onion**

1. To make the chile salsa, fill a medium-size pot halfway with water and add the tomatoes, chiles, jalapeño, and garlic. Cook over medium heat for 8 to 10 minutes, or until the vegetables become soft. Using a slotted spoon, transfer the cooked vegetables to a blender and add the onion, 1 cup (240 ml) reserved cooking water, and the spices. Blend until smooth.

2. In a large skillet over medium-high heat, heat 3 to 4 tablespoons (45 to 60 ml) of the oil until hot. Add the steak and let it cook for 1 to 2 minutes to build color. Stir the steak so all sides are browned, sprinkle in the flour, and cook for 2 to 3 minutes, stirring often.

3. Once the flour is cooked, add the blended chile salsa and stir well to incorporate. Cover the skillet and adjust the heat to maintain a simmer. Cook for about 1 hour, or until the sauce thickens, stirring every few minutes. You may need to add water to thin the sauce the way you like it if it becomes too thick. Taste and add salt and pepper as needed.

4. On a plancha over medium heat, warm the tortillas for 10 to 15 seconds per side. Spoon a couple tablespoons (about 28 g) of the guisado de res into each taco. Top with cilantro and onion and serve immediately.

# SMOKED CHICKEN ENCHILADA CASSEROLE

This chicken enchilada casserole is one of the best uses of leftover smoked chicken, or even Thanksgiving Smoked Turkey Breast (page 101) as an alternative to turkey sandwiches for the next week. Use freshly shredded cheeses, as they melt and taste better than commercially packaged shredded cheese. This casserole makes a lot of food, which you can portion and freeze for up to six months if desired. You can opt for canned enchilada sauce with this recipe, but I highly suggest making it from scratch if you have the time, as it elevates the dish with a ton more flavor.

## FOR ENCHILADA SAUCE

3 tablespoons (45 ml) canola oil

3 tablespoons (23.25 g) all-purpose flour

1 tablespoon (7.5 g) dark chili powder

1 teaspoon ground cumin

½ teaspoon kosher salt

½ teaspoon ground black pepper

½ teaspoon dried Mexican oregano

¼ teaspoon ground cinnamon

2 tablespoons (32 g) tomato paste

2 cups (480 ml) vegetable stock

1 teaspoon apple cider vinegar

## FOR CHICKEN FILLING

3 cups (711 g) shredded smoked chicken

1 cup (240 g) Mexican crema or sour cream, plus more for garnish

1 (10-ounce, or 280 g) can diced tomatoes with green chilies, drained

1 (4-ounce, or 115 g) can diced green chilies, drained

½ cup (8 g) fresh cilantro, chopped, plus more for garnish

1 tablespoon (10 g) kosher salt

1 teaspoon ground black pepper

1 teaspoon granulated garlic

1 teaspoon dark chili powder

½ teaspoon ground cumin

15 (6-inch, or 15 cm) corn tortillas

3 cups (360 g) freshly shredded Monterrey Jack cheese

CONTINUED ➤➤

1. Preheat the oven to 375°F (190°C, or gas mark 5).

2. To prepare the enchilada sauce, in a medium-size pot over medium-low heat, heat the oil. Add the flour and the spices to the hot oil (it should sizzle or it's not hot enough). Whisk to incorporate and cook for 1 to 2 minutes until fragrant. Add the tomato paste and continue whisking until smooth.

3. Slowly pour in the stock and whisk to remove any lumps in the sauce. Raise the heat slightly so the sauce simmers, then reduce the heat to low and cook for 6 to 7 minutes, or until the sauce thickens slightly. Remove from the heat and stir in the vinegar.

4. Coat a 9 × 13-inch (23 × 33 cm) baking dish with butter or nonstick cooking spray.

5. To prepare the casserole, in a large bowl, combine the chicken, half of the enchilada sauce, the crema, tomatoes and green chilies, diced green chilies, cilantro, and spices. Mix well with a spatula.

6. Drizzle the bottom of the prepared baking dish with some of the remaining enchilada sauce until it's well coated. Layer 5 corn tortillas on the sauce, then spoon about one-third of the chicken mixture on top and spread it out with a spatula. Drizzle enchilada sauce on the chicken mixture, then sprinkle on 1 cup (120 g) of the cheese. Repeat two more times to create three layers total.

7. Cover the dish tightly with aluminum foil and bake for 25 minutes. Remove the foil and bake for 10 minutes longer, or until the cheese is bubbly. Remove the casserole from the oven and let it cool for 10 to 15 minutes to set.

8. Garnish with Mexican crema drizzled over the top and chopped cilantro. Serve immediately.

# PORK BELLY BRISKET TACOS

Pork belly and brisket don't normally fall into the same sentence unless you're at a restaurant that serves them both. But pork belly *cooked like a brisket*? That's blasphemy, right? Wrong! Pork belly brisket takes everything we know in Texas about smoking that perfectly peppery, barked-up brisket and applies it to succulent pork belly. This dish is rich, almost like eating wagyu. It goes without saying that putting something this good in a taco is a must-have in Tex-Mex barbecue, but it's elevated even more with the nontraditional toppings. So, next time you're in the mood for brisket, try pork belly instead. Your friends and family will thank you!

1 boneless, skinless pork belly, cut into thirds

1 cup (136 g) coarse black pepper

⅓ cup (75 g) packed light brown sugar

¼ cup (40 g) kosher salt

¼ cup (58 g) seasoned salt

¼ cup (40 g) granulated garlic

¼ cup (30 g) dark chili powder

2 cups (480 ml) apple cider vinegar

2 cups (480 ml) water

12 (4½-inch, or 11 cm) corn tortillas

1 cup (240 g) Cilantro Lime Crema (page 47)

1 cup (167 g) Spicy Pickled Red Onions (page 62)

1 cup (16 g) chopped fresh cilantro

1. Preheat a smoker to 225°F (107°C) using pecan or post oak wood. We're starting it lower to get more smoke on the pork belly, much like we would a brisket.

2. Trim the pork belly pieces to they are symmetrically shaped rectangles. Trim away any sections that are mostly fat and aren't uniform.

3. In a medium-size bowl, stir together the pepper, brown sugar, kosher salt, seasoned salt, granulated garlic, and chili powder. Season both sides of the pork belly pieces liberally with the spices. Place the pork belly in the smoker and cook for 3 to 4 hours until it starts to achieve the peppery bark that Texas brisket is known for. Combine the vinegar and water in a spritz bottle.

4. Increase the heat to 250°F (120°C). Continue to cook for 1½ to 2 hours until the pork belly reaches 180°F to 185°F (82°C to 85°C), spritzing it once every hour with the vinegar-water solution. Wrap the pork tightly in butcher paper like you would a brisket (see page 145) and place it back in the smoker. Cook for 1 to 2 hours longer until it reaches an internal temperature between 200°F and 205°F (93°C and 96°C), or until the belly probes like butter. Remove from the smoker.

5. To build your tacos, on a medium-hot plancha, warm the tortillas for 10 to 15 seconds per side.

6. Slice the pork belly with a serrated knife and layer on 2 slices per taco. Drizzle with the crema and garnish with pickled red onions and cilantro. Serve immediately.

# SMOKED TACOS DE LENGA

Lengua (cow's tongue) is an incredible dish in Mexican cuisine when done right. In fact, I grew up eating lengua from Danal's restaurant in Irving, Texas, without ever knowing it came from a cow's tongue. It's rich and decadent, like barbacoa, but has almost a chopped brisket mouthfeel. I love this recipe because it takes one of my favorite things to eat as a kid and adds a layer of complexity to it by smoking the lengua after boiling it. This pairs perfectly with a homemade guacamole and my Smoky Salsa Roja (page 44).

**1 beef tongue (2 to 3 pounds, or 908 g to 1.3 kg)**
**4 garlic cloves, peeled**
**1 white onion, halved**
**2 bay leaves**
**1 tablespoon (10 g) kosher salt**
**1 tablespoon (6 g) ground black pepper**
**1 teaspoon ground cumin**
**1 teaspoon smoked paprika**
**1 teaspoon dried Mexican oregano**
**1 teaspoon dark chili powder**
**¼ cup (60 ml) canola oil**
**½ cup (about 115 g) Hurtado Beef Blend (page 28)**
**12 (4½-inch, or 11 cm) corn tortillas**
**1 cup (260 g) Smoky Salsa Roja (page 44)**
**Chopped fresh cilantro, for garnish**

## FOR GUACAMOLE
**3 ripe avocados, halved and pitted**
**1 tablespoon (10 g) kosher salt**
**½ cup (120 ml) fresh lime juice**
**½ cup (90 g) diced Roma tomato**
**½ cup (80 g) diced red onion**
**¼ cup (38 g) diced jalapeño pepper**
**¼ cup (4 g) chopped fresh cilantro**
**1 tablespoon (10 g) minced garlic**
**1 teaspoon chopped sun-dried tomato**
**1 teaspoon ground black pepper**
**½ teaspoon ground cumin**
**½ teaspoon granulated garlic**

1. Fill a medium-size pot halfway with water and bring it to a boil over high heat. Add the beef tongue, garlic, onion, bay leaves, salt, pepper, cumin, smoked paprika, oregano, and chili powder. Turn the heat medium-low and cook covered for 2 to 3 hours, or until the tongue probes tender. Remove the tongue from the pot and let it cool for a few minutes. Peel the skin from the tongue using a sharp knife (it should come off easily, if it's tender).

2. Preheat a smoker to 250°F (120°C).

3. Rub the beef tongue with the oil and season with the beef blend. Place the tongue in the smoker and cook for 2 to 3 hours, or until it reaches an internal temperature of 185°F (85°C).

4. To prepare the guacamole, while the tongue smokes, scoop the avocado flesh into a large bowl and add the salt and lime juice. Mix and mash the avocado until it no longer has large chunks in it. With a spatula, fold in the Roma tomato, onion, jalapeño, cilantro, minced garlic, sun-dried tomato, pepper, cumin, and granulated garlic. Set aside.

5. On a hot plancha, toast the tortillas for 10 to 12 seconds per side.

6. To build your tacos, spoon about 1 tablespoon (16 g) of the salsa roja across each tortilla.

7. Slice or chop the beef tongue and top each taco with about 3½ ounces (100 g) of the meat. Add a dollop of guacamole and garnish with cilantro. Serve immediately.

# LEGENDS OF TEX-MEX BARBECUE:
# ERNEST SERVANTES

"Barbecue is about as hard as it gets. I live by two words: sacrifice and discipline. You have to make sacrifices and be disciplined. At the end of the day, you also need grit. Barbecue is about as pure as a cuisine gets, because you use fire, not natural gas or ovens. It's primordial—very caveman-like—using fire to control the food. It's not throwing meat in the pit, setting the temperature at 350°F (180°C), and it's done in a couple of hours. You've got to add the wood and go through rain, snow, wind, and humidity. There are lots of variables to understand when making the perfect brisket. People often tell me they can do it, and I say, 'Yes, you can make one, but can you make seventy in one shot? And they all come out consistently good?'

"Everybody in Texas takes pride in being from Texas, and we think we cook the best barbecue in the land. Texas barbecue resonates and inspires because of its hundreds of years of tradition, taken from the cowboys and vaqueros of the 1800s, who cooked what they had. We keep it simple so you can taste the meat. The saying in Texas is if you have to use barbecue sauce, you're hiding something.

"The Burnt Bean Company has been a dream of mine since day one. I wanted to become the best barbecue restaurant in the state of Texas, in the country. I tell people I'm only as good as the next brisket I cook.

"I wanted to tell my story through cooking; this is my soul food. It tells stories from the sides to the condiments; everything is a memory of my upraising. From my grandfather's pickled okra to my grandmother's and mom's recipes to my father's way of cooking brisket and barbecue, I'm sharing my family's story through food. I'm welcoming you to my house when we barbecue. That's what I do. I carry on the legacy of my family."

*—Ernest Servantes,*
*Burnt Bean Co. Barbecue,*
*Seguin, Texas*

# GRILLED LOBSTER TOSTADAS

This lobster tostada is neither traditional barbecue nor Tex-Mex. In fact, it's got more of an Asian flair with miso, ginger, and scallion, but it's one of the best things I've ever made, and you'll be glad you tried it (and surprised at how easy it is to make). This is the perfect appetizer for parties, or even a plated dinner if you're entertaining.

## FOR COMPOUND BUTTER

**1 cup (2 sticks, or 224 g) unsalted butter, at room temperature**
**1 tablespoon (4 g) fresh tarragon, chopped**
**1 teaspoon fresh chopped parsley**
**1 teaspoon minced garlic**
**1 teaspoon grated lemon zest**
**½ teaspoon kosher salt**
**½ teaspoon red chili flakes**
**½ teaspoon black pepper**

## FOR THE LOBSTER

**1 pound (454 g) lobster tails (about 2 tails)**
**1 tablespoon (15 ml) rice wine vinegar**
**1 teaspoon garlic paste**
**1 teaspoon ginger paste**
**1 teaspoon sesame oil**
**1 teaspoon fresh lemon juice**
**1 teaspoon kosher salt**
**1 teaspoon ground black pepper**
**1 Persian cucumber, very thinly sliced**
**¼ cup (60 ml) water**
**2 tablespoons (34 g) miso paste**
**2 cups (480 ml) canola oil**
**½ cup (58 g) very thinly sliced shallots**
**6 mini tostada shells**
**1 avocado, peeled, halved, pitted, and thinly sliced**

1. Preheat a grill using lump charcoal with pecan or hickory wood chunks.

2. To prepare the compound butter, in a large bowl, combine all the ingredients and use a spatula to mix well. Set aside at room temperature with a brush to baste with.

3. Prepare the lobster tails by cutting down the top of the tails with a pair of kitchen shears and pulling the meat through so it's exposed, leaving the shells intact.

4. Once the grill is hot, carefully set the lobster tails on the grill and cook for 5 to 6 minutes, basting with the compound butter every 1 to 2 minutes. When the lobster is bright red and cooked through, remove it from the heat. Remove the lobster meat from the shells, discard the shells, and chop the meat into ½-inch (1 cm) chunks. In a medium-size bowl, stir together the lobster and any remaining compound butter.

5. In another medium-size bowl, whisk the vinegar, garlic, ginger, sesame oil, lemon juice, salt, and pepper. Add the cucumber to the bowl, toss to combine, and refrigerate until needed.

6. In a small bowl, whisk the water and miso paste to blend.

CONTINUED ➤➤

7. In a small pot over medium-high heat, heat canola oil until hot. Carefully add the shallots and fry for 8 to 10 minutes, or until golden brown. Transfer to paper towel to drain and crisp.

8. To build the tostadas, spread 1 tablespoon (15 ml) of the miso mixture across each tostada. Top with 2 or 3 seasoned cucumber slices. Carefully spoon lobster chunks over each tostada, dividing the meat evenly. Finish by spooning some of the cucumber juice over the lobster and garnishing with 2 to 3 avocado slices and crispy shallots. Serve immediately.

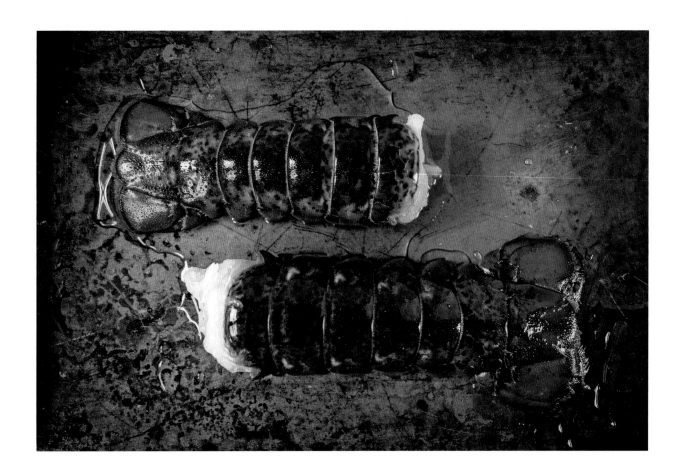

# PICADILLO PUFFY TACOS

San Antonio is the epicenter of the puffy taco. Places like Ray's, Mi Tierra, and Pico de Gallo are some of the most memorable Tex-Mex experiences I had as a kid travel-ing through San Antonio to the Texas Gulf Coast with my family. What makes a good puffy taco? Scratch-made corn tortillas, first off. You have to achieve the ultimate puffiness and can only do that with a hand-pressed tortilla. (If you don't have a tortilla press, you can buy raw flour tortillas from most grocery stores and fry that in lieu of corn, for an equally crunchy puffy taco.) Secondly, you need a damn good picadillo, with sautéed potatoes in the ground beef and enough chili powder for that deep, rich color picadillo is known for. Lastly, freshly shredded cheddar cheese sets off these tacos. Don't be lazy and settle for packaged shredded cheese, full of antibinding agents. Cheddar is better when it's freshly shredded!

## FOR PICADILLO

¼ cup (60 ml) canola oil
1 pound (454 g) ground beef
1 Yukon gold potato, diced
½ white onion, diced
¼ cup (38 g) diced jalapeño pepper
1 tablespoon (16 g) tomato paste
¼ cup (60 ml) water
1 tablespoon (7.5 g) dark chili powder
1 teaspoon smoked paprika
1 teaspoon granulated garlic
1 teaspoon kosher salt
1 teaspoon ground black pepper
½ teaspoon ground cumin

## FOR HOMEMADE CORN TORTILLAS

2 cups (252 g) masa harina (corn flour)
½ teaspoon kosher salt
1¼ cups (300 ml) warm water
4 cups (960 ml) vegetable oil

## FOR TOPPINGS

2 cups (85 g) shredded lettuce
½ cup (90 g) diced tomato
2 cups (240 g) freshly shredded cheddar cheese

CONTINUED ▶▶

1. To prepare the picadillo, heat a medium-size skillet over medium-high heat. Add the canola oil and ground beef and cook for 2 to 3 minutes. Stir the beef and add the potato. Continue to cook for 4 to 5 minutes, stirring every minute or so. Stir in the onion, jalapeño, and tomato paste. Cook for 2 to 3 minutes, stirring occasionally, then add the water and spices. Adjust the heat to maintain a simmer and cook for 8 to 10 minutes.

2. To prepare the tortillas, in a medium-size bowl, whisk the masa harina and salt to combine, then pour in the water and mix until a dough forms. Roll the dough into golf ball–size portions.

3. Using a tortilla press, place a dough ball between two pieces of parchment paper and press into a tortilla. Repeat with the remaining dough balls.

4. In a medium-size pot over medium-high heat, heat the vegetable oil to 350°F (180°C). Carefully place a raw tortilla in the hot oil and use a spatula to press the middle of the tortilla, forming a "puffy taco" around the spatula. Fry for 1 to 2 minutes, then flip and cook the top for 1 to 2 minutes. Carefully transfer the tortilla to a wire rack to cool, placing it upside-down on the rack. Repeat with the remaining tortillas.

5. To plate, spoon 4 ounces (115 g) of the picadillo into a puffy taco shell. Top with ½ cup (11 g) of the shredded lettuce. Garnish with diced tomato and cheese and serve immediately.

# PULLED PORK COSTRA TACOS

This is the ultimate keto taco, with a crunchy, cheesy shell that is fast and easy to make. Costra tacos work well with any protein, but especially so with pulled pork. The spicy barbecue sauce cuts through the richness of the fatty pork and the crispy, cheesy taco shell. For a less greasy taco shell, flip them upside-down on a metal taco shell rack and bake them in a 350°F (180°C, or gas mark 4) oven for 4 to 5 minutes until crispy.

---

**2 cups (240 g) shredded cheddar cheese**

**1 cup (120 g) shredded Colby Jack cheese**

**1 cup (240 ml) Original Rib Glaze (page 37)**

**½ cup (120 ml) hot sauce (such as Valentina)**

**1 pound (454 g) cooked Tex-Mex Pulled Pork (page 108), warmed through**

**Chopped fresh cilantro, for garnish**

**Chopped white onion, for garnish**

1. Preheat a griddle or plancha over medium-high heat.

2. In a large bowl, combine the cheeses and toss them to mix. Carefully place ½ cup (60 g) of the cheese mixture on the hot griddle in a circle about 4½ inches (11 cm) in diameter. Let the cheese cook for 2 to 3 minutes, or until golden brown underneath, then flip and cook for 1 to 2 minutes longer.

3. In a medium-size bowl, stir together the rib glaze and hot sauce to make a spicy barbecue sauce.

4. Fill each cheese "tortilla" with 5 to 6 ounces (140 to 170 g) of the pulled pork, then drizzle the spicy barbecue sauce over them. Garnish with cilantro and onion to serve.

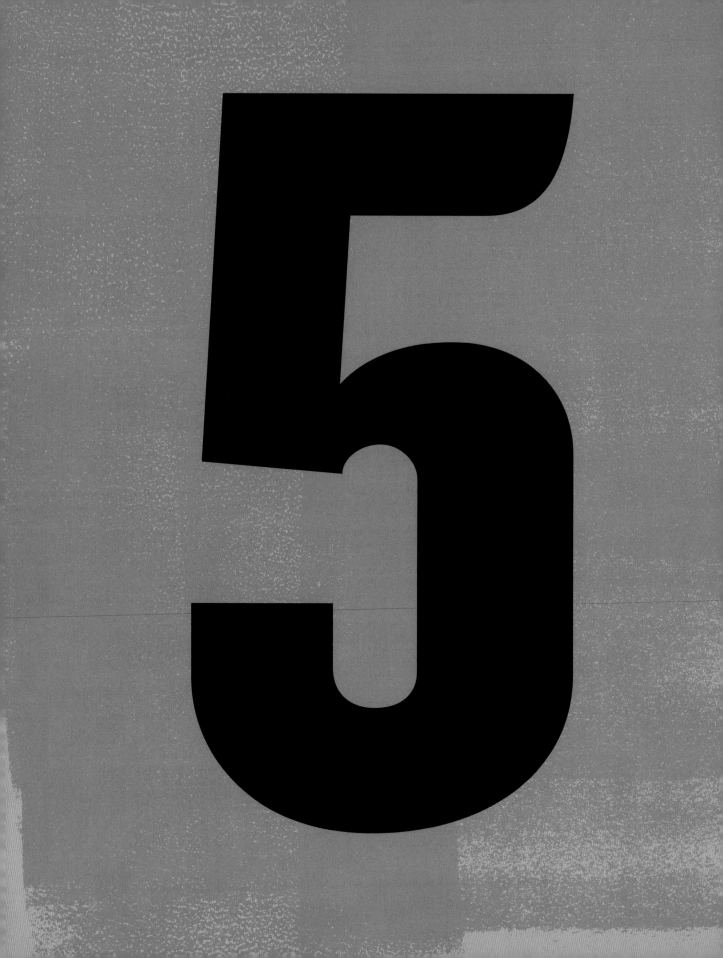

# BREAK-FAST

# BREAKFAST IS THE MOST

important meal of the day, and by that I mean it could be *any meal of the day*. I love everything about what breakfast embodies. It's a blank canvas for combining eggs and potatoes, or chorizo with gravy. Walking into a kitchen in the early morning hours and smelling the sharp pork fat from bacon sizzling or jalapeños roasting for salsa is a smell you won't soon forget. My favorite recipe in this book, hands down, is the brisket migas (page 181), and I hope you'll enjoy these recipes as much as I've enjoyed making them for my family at home.

# JALAPEÑO CORN BREAD WAFFLES

When I started the brick-and-mortar location in 2020, I wanted to stray from the classic corn bread most barbecue joints offer and venture into a side item that held true to my heritage. So, I played around with corn bread muffins filled with jalapeño, onion, cheese, and even brisket. My mom made a similar corn bread when I was younger that we called "Mexican corn bread" and it usually had ground beef in it. My Mexican Corn Bread Muffins (page 139) were an instant hit in the restaurant, especially when topped with honey and butter while fresh from the oven. It was the ultimate sweet, smoky, spicy, savory corn bread. Fast-forward a couple years to a waffle iron left over from a restaurant we purchased. One day, our pitmaster, John, texted me to come try a new breakfast item he created: the batter from our corn bread muffins plopped into a buttered waffle iron. The result was one of the most glorious things I've ever eaten for breakfast. We still top the waffle with honey and butter, just like the muffins, but its texture is unmatched. Thank you, John!

**4 cups (624) corn bread mix**
**1 teaspoon baking powder**
**1 teaspoon granulated sugar**
**1 teaspoon kosher salt**
**1 cup (240 ml) water**
**¼ cup (60 ml) canola oil**
**6 tablespoons (84 g) unsalted butter, melted**
**½ cup (60 g) shredded cheddar cheese**
**½ cup (83 g) frozen corn kernels**
**¼ cup (38 g) diced jalapeño pepper**
**¼ cup (40 g) diced white onion**
**¼ cup (4 g) chopped fresh cilantro**
**6 ounces (170 g) chopped Tex-Mex Smoked Brisket (page 89), or store-bought**
**Butter, softened, for serving**
**Honey, for serving**

1. In a large mixing bowl, whisk the corn bread mix, baking powder, sugar, and salt to combine well. Add the water, oil, and melted butter. Whisk until smooth.

2. Add the cheese, vegetables, cilantro, and brisket to the batter and fold it in with a spatula.

3. Preheat a waffle iron to 375°F (190°C). Spray it heavily with nonstick cooking spray.

4. Pour ½ cup (57 g) of the batter into the preheated waffle iron and cook for 3 to 4 minutes, or until the waffle is crispy around the edges and cooked all the way through. Repeat with the remaining batter.

5. Serve immediately topped with a dollop of butter and a drizzle with honey.

# LEGENDS OF
# TEX-MEX BARBECUE:
# ESAUL RAMOS JR.

"As a kid, I wasn't drawn to cooking. Every weekend, my dad barbecued, and I just liked fire. I finally took over because the meat would burn because dad and my uncles had such a good time. Out of high school, I worked in a Cajun restaurant and then at La Barbecue in Austin for two years to learn from my mentor, John Lewis. After Austin was Mexico to stage (intern) at little taquerias, and make salsa and tortillas with my aunts. Then to Utah to master working on a cooker and to the Carolinas for pork and hogs. I worked for free, getting paid with knowledge.

"Back in San Antonio, I found a restaurant for sale on Craigslist. My best friend and business partner, Joe, and I didn't have money, but we made a handshake deal with the owner: after a year, we purchase the place or he could kick us out. Eight years later, our restaurant 2M Smokehouse is still there.

"Growing up, my grandmother and mother made great food, and those flavors stuck in my head. My Mexican grandmother's recipes inspired me and my U.S.-born mother introduced me to Tex-Mex. So, I combined their cooking with barbecue and, at that time, the pairing was unique.

"Many people say they want to do what I do, and anyone can. But if you have a plan B, you've already failed. Barbecue is what I love and every single morning it is all I want to do. You don't need money to succeed; just strap your boots up and work. Nothing but death should stop you from achieving what you want.

"I met Brandon Hurtado at the height of the COVID pandemic at a pop-up barbecue joint. He was barely starting and what he's done is impressive. As much as he says I inspired him, he's been a ginormous inspiration to me. His whole entire business model and what he's accomplished is awesome. He's one of the reasons for the new business model at my new restaurant Blu Lacy in Castroville. I'm trying to be more of a businessman while keeping passion for the food. Eventually, though, I want to retire and cook brisket once a year for my family and friends."

**—Esaul Ramos Jr., 2M Smokehouse,
San Antonio, Texas**

# BRISKET BENEDICT

One of the simple pleasures in life is a good eggs Benedict. My brisket benny is simple, straightforward, and a little spicy thanks to the hot sauce drizzle at the end. The smokiness from the brisket carries through in every bite, and there's no substitute for a perfectly poached egg, so make sure to set a timer. This recipe doesn't use English muffins; in fact, I much prefer my homemade flaky biscuits as a base.

## FOR HOLLANDAISE SAUCE

**3 large egg yolks**
**1 tablespoon (15 ml) fresh lemon juice**
**8 tablespoons (1 stick, or 112 g) unsalted butter, melted**
**Kosher salt**
**Ground black pepper**

## FOR POACHED EGGS

**1 tablespoon (15 ml) white vinegar**
**4 large eggs**

## FOR BENEDICT

**2 Buttermilk Biscuits (see Chorizo Biscuits and Gravy, page 182) or store-bought, halved**
**6 ounces (170 g) sliced Tex-Mex Smoked Brisket (page 89), or store-bought**
**¼ cup (60 ml) hot sauce (such as Valentina)**
**1 tablespoon (1 g) chopped fresh cilantro**

1. Have a pot of simmering water on the stovetop (for the double boiler method for the hollandaise sauce).

2. To prepare the hollandaise sauce, in a medium-size heat-resistant bowl, whisk the egg yolks and lemon juice until well combined. Place the bowl over the simmering water and cook for 2 to 3 minutes, whisking, until the mixture thickens. Slowly drizzle in the melted butter while whisking and cook for 2 to 3 minutes longer until the sauce is smooth and thickened. Season to taste with salt and pepper. Keep the sauce warm in a low oven.

3. To poach the eggs, fill a medium-size pot halfway with water and bring it to a boil over high heat. Add the vinegar.

4. Crack an egg into a small ramekin and set aside. Using a slotted spoon, swirl the water in the pot in a circle 2 to 3 times, creating a whirlpool, then carefully pour the egg into the swirling water. Cook for 3 to 4 minutes, or until the egg white is set and the yolk is still runny. Carefully remove the egg with the slotted spoon and repeat the process with the remaining eggs.

5. To assemble, place the biscuit halves on individual plates and top each with brisket. Top the brisket with a poached egg. Spoon hollandaise sauce across the egg and drizzle with hot sauce. Garnish with cilantro and enjoy.

# PORK BELLY PANCAKES

You may have had bacon with pancakes, but have you ever had bacon burnt ends with them? Who doesn't love a good sweet-and-savory combination for breakfast? This recipe doesn't just call for burnt ends atop your flapjacks, though. I like to chop the burnt ends and put them in the pancake batter so every bite contains that sweet, smoky pork belly flavor with hints of Mexican vanilla from the agave syrup. Try this recipe and you won't go back to regular cured bacon with your pancakes—I promise!

1½ cups (186 g) all-purpose flour

3½ teaspoons (16 g) baking powder

1 tablespoon (12.5 g) granulated sugar

1 teaspoon kosher salt

1¼ cups (300 ml) milk

1 large egg

3 tablespoons (45 ml) melted butter, plus more for the griddle

1 pound (454 g) cooked Pork Belly Burnt Ends (page 97)

2 cups (480 ml) agave nectar

1 cinnamon stick

1 teaspoon Mexican vanilla extract

½ teaspoon cayenne pepper

Powdered sugar, for garnish

1. In a large bowl, whisk the flour, baking powder, sugar, and salt to combine.

2. In another large bowl, whisk the milk, egg, and melted butter until blended. Pour the wet ingredients into the dry ingredients and gently stir until combined.

3. Roughly chop half of the burnt ends and fold them into the pancake batter.

4. Heat a nonstick griddle or flattop over medium heat and grease it with butter or nonstick cooking spray.

5. Pour ⅓ cup (38 g) of batter onto the griddle for each pancake. Cook for 1½ to 2 minutes until the pancakes begin to bubble on top, then flip and cook for 60 to 90 seconds until golden brown. Remove the pancakes from the griddle and set aside in a warmer or low oven. Repeat with the remaining batter.

6. In a small saucepan over low to medium heat, combine the agave nectar, cinnamon stick, vanilla, and cayenne. Heat for about 5 minutes, stirring occasionally, until warmed and combined.

7. Place 3 to 4 of the remaining burnt ends on each pancake. Drizzle the agave syrup across the burnt ends and garnish with powdered sugar.

# BRISKET MIGAS

Hands down, this is my favorite recipe in this entire book. It's simple, spicy, and savory all at once. Migas is a dish I make for my wife and kids on a weekly basis for breakfast. Heck, we eat migas for lunch or dinner sometimes because of how quick, easy, and delicious it is. I call for my Smoked Salsa Verde (page 43) here, but you can also use Smoky Salsa Roja (page 44) to kick it up a notch. Always, and I mean always, fry your own tortilla chips. There's no substitute for freshly fried corn tortilla chips hit with a little seasoned salt or chile lime seasoning.

½ cup (120 ml) canola oil

6 (6-inch, or 15 cm) corn tortillas, cut into 1½-inch (3.5 cm) squares

½ teaspoon seasoned salt

⅓ cup (43 g) Smoked Salsa Verde (page 43)

2 large eggs

4 ounces (115 g) chopped Tex-Mex Smoked Brisket (page 89), or store-bought

¼ cup (4 g) chopped fresh cilantro, plus more for garnish

½ cup (60 g) shredded cheddar cheese

2 tablespoons (14 g) shredded Cotija cheese

¼ cup (60 g) Mexican crema

**I.** In a large skillet or deep pot over medium-high heat, heat the oil. Add the tortilla squares and fry for 5 to 6 minutes, stirring occasionally, until the chips are crispy. Season with the seasoned salt.

**2.** In a separate cast iron skillet, add the salsa verde and eggs. Cook for 2 to 3 minutes, stirring constantly, or until the eggs begin to firm up.

**3.** Add the brisket and cilantro, folding them into the mixture.

**4.** Add the cheddar cheese and continue to cook, gently folding the migas, for 1 to 2 minutes until melted. Turn off the heat.

**5.** Plate the migas and sprinkle with the Cotija cheese. Drizzle with the crema and garnish with cilantro. Serve immediately with tortilla chips.

# CHORIZO BISCUITS AND GRAVY

Biscuits and gravy may have originated in southern Appalachia, but they're taken to new heights when combined with Mexican chorizo-infused cream gravy. This dish is one of those breakfasts you don't eat every day, but it's worth it when you do!

---

## FOR BUTTERMILK BISCUITS

2 cups (248 g) all-purpose flour, plus more for dusting

1 tablespoon (14 g) baking powder

½ teaspoon kosher salt

8 tablespoons (1 stick, or 112 g) cold unsalted butter, cut into small chunks

¾ cup (180 ml) cold buttermilk

Melted butter, for brushing (optional)

## FOR CHORIZO GRAVY

8 ounces (225 g) Mexican chorizo

1 teaspoon smoked paprika

½ teaspoon ground cumin

½ teaspoon ground black pepper, plus more as needed

1 tablespoon (14 g) unsalted butter

2 tablespoons (15.5 g) all-purpose flour

½ cup (120 ml) heavy whipping cream

2 cups (480 ml) whole milk

Kosher salt

1. Preheat the oven to 425°F (220°C, or gas mark 7). Line a baking sheet with parchment paper.

2. To prepare the biscuits, in a large bowl, whisk the flour, baking powder, and salt to combine. Add the cold butter cubes and use a pastry cutter, or two forks, to cut the butter into the flour until it resembles crumbs. Make a well in the center of the flour mixture and pour in the cold buttermilk. Stir the mixture together with a fork until a dough forms, but be sure not to overmix the dough.

3. Lightly dust a work surface with flour and transfer the dough to it. Knead the dough into a ball for 4 to 5 minutes.

4. Using a rolling pin, roll the dough into a ½-inch (1 cm) thick square. With a biscuit cutter, cut 6 to 8 biscuits from the dough. Place the biscuits on the prepared baking sheet about 1 inch (2.5 cm) apart.

5. Bake for 12 to 15 minutes, or until golden brown. Remove from the oven and brush the top with melted butter (if using). Set aside.

6. To prepare the chorizo gravy, heat a medium-size cast-iron skillet or sauté pan over medium-high heat. Add the chorizo and cook for 5 to 6 minutes until it starts to brown, stirring occasionally.

7. Stir in the smoked paprika, cumin, and pepper. Cook for 2 to 3 minutes, then stir in the butter and flour. Cook the chorizo and flour for another 2 to 3 minutes, stirring occasionally, until the flour begins to form a paste.

8. Pour in the heavy cream and stir to incorporate. Cook for 4 to 5 minutes until the cream begins to thicken, then pour in the milk, a little at a time, stirring occasionally. Turn the heat to low and let the gravy cook for 3 to 4 minutes until it thickens. Taste and season with salt and more pepper as needed.

9. To plate, serve the warm biscuits whole and ladle the chorizo gravy over the biscuits.

# BRISKET BREAKFAST TACOS

Candied jalapeños are not the norm when it comes to brisket, or breakfast tacos, but they're the perfect accompaniment to this nontraditional take on a classic taco. Our tortillas come from a small tortilleria in Oak Cliff, Texas, and have the perfect amount of lard (fat) in them so they bubble and puff on the plancha when heated. I love how they're thin and pliable, so you can pile on a ton of eggs and brisket without them breaking.

## FOR CANDIED JALAPEÑOS

2 cups (400 g) granulated sugar

1 cup (240 ml) apple cider vinegar

½ teaspoon garlic powder

½ teaspoon ground turmeric

½ teaspoon celery seed

½ teaspoon mustard seed

1 pound (454 g) jalapeño peppers, sliced ¼-inch (0.6 cm) thick

## FOR BREAKFAST BRISKET TACOS

4 large eggs

½ cup (120 ml) heavy whipping cream

4 tablespoons (½ stick, or 56 g) unsalted butter

Kosher salt

Ground black pepper

1 cup (120 g) shredded cheddar cheese

6 (6-inch, or 15 cm) flour tortillas (Sonoran-style, if you can find them)

1 pound (454 g) chopped Tex-Mex Smoked Brisket (page 89), or store-bought, warmed through

½ cup (64 g) Smoked Salsa Verde (page 43)

¼ cup (4 g) chopped fresh cilantro

1. To prepare the candied jalapeños, in a small pot over medium heat, combine the sugar, vinegar, and spices and bring to a boil. Add the jalapeños. Cook for 4 to 5 minutes, or until the jalapeños change color and become soft. Reserve ½ cup (65 g) of the candied jalapeños for the tacos. Transfer the remaining jalapeños to a Mason jar, seal the jar, and keep refrigerated for up to 3 to 4 months.

2. To prepare the tacos, in a medium-size bowl, whisk the eggs and heavy cream to blend.

3. Place a skillet over medium heat and add the butter to melt. Pour in the eggs and cook for 3 to 4 minutes, stirring constantly, until the eggs begin to curdle. Season to taste with salt and pepper and continue to cook for 2 to 3 minutes longer, stirring. Remove from the heat and gently fold in the cheddar cheese.

4. On a plancha or griddle over medium heat, heat the tortillas for 15 to 20 seconds per side, flipping 3 to 4 times.

5. To build the tacos, spoon the cheesy scrambled eggs onto the tortillas. Top with the chopped brisket and spoon salsa over the brisket. Finish by adding 2 or 3 candied jalapeño slices to each taco and garnish with the cilantro.

# BRISKET BISCUIT

The brisket biscuit is a Fort Worth breakfast icon. It started with my buddy Derek Allan, who operated Derek Allan's Texas Barbecue for years before graciously allowing me to take over his spot in 2022. One of the things I promised to continue was serving breakfast to the local community, which is something I don't do at my other locations. The brisket biscuit torch was then passed with a slight Tex-Mex variation—the addition of salsa.

2 tablespoons (28 g) butter

2 large eggs

2 Buttermilk Biscuits (see Chorizo Biscuits and Gravy, page 182) or store-bought, halved

8 ounces (225 g) sliced Tex-Mex Smoked Brisket (page 89), or store-bought, warmed through

2 slices American cheese

¼ cup (32 g) Smoked Salsa Verde (page 43)

1. Place a sauté pan or skillet over medium heat. Add the butter to melt and swirl it to coat the entire pan.

2. In a medium-size bowl, whisk the eggs until the whites and yolks are combined.

3. Once the butter begins to foam in the pan, add the eggs and cook for 3 to 4 minutes, stirring constantly, making sure to scrape the sides and bottom of the pan, until the eggs begin to curdle. Continue to cook, stirring, for 2 to 3 minutes longer, or until the eggs are creamy. Remove from the heat.

4. Place the sliced brisket on the biscuits' bottom halves, dividing it evenly.

5. Spoon the scrambled eggs onto the brisket and place a slice of cheese over the eggs.

6. Drizzle the salsa verde over the cheese and place the other biscuit half on top. Serve immediately.

# SMOKED MENUDO

Menudo has a love-hate relationship with folks across north Texas. They either love it, or love to hate it, because of the tripe (cow intestine) that serves as the main ingredient. My Grandma Nico made the best damn menudo when I was growing up, and she didn't overcomplicate it: tripe, hominy, soup, limes, onion, and homemade flour tortillas. My dad could eat a gallon of it all by himself! This recipe has a smoky element (because, why not?) thanks to the addition of smoked beef tallow, which gives the menudo a creamy, smoky finish that coats the roof of your mouth in the best way possible.

2 tablespoons (30 ml) canola oil

4 garlic cloves, minced

2 pounds (908 g) beef tripe, cleaned and cut into 1-inch (2.5 cm) pieces

1 pound (454 g) beef feet, cleaned and cut into small chunks

1 white onion, quartered

2 tablespoons (14 g) smoked paprika

2 tablespoons (15 g) dark chili powder

1 tablespoon (10 g) kosher salt

2 teaspoons dried Mexican oregano

2 teaspoons ground cumin

1 teaspoon ground black pepper

8 cups (1.9 L) beef stock

8 ounces (225 g) smoked beef tallow

2 cups (480 ml) water

2 (15-ounce, or 425 g) cans hominy, rinsed and drained

## FOR SERVING

Diced white onion

Chopped fresh cilantro

Lime wedges

Flour tortillas

1. In a large pot over medium heat, heat the oil. Add the garlic and sauté for 1 to 2 minutes until fragrant. Add the beef tripe and beef feet to the pot and cook for 4 to 5 minutes, or until browned on all sides.

2. Add the onion, smoked paprika, chili powder, salt, oregano, cumin, and pepper to the pot. Stir to coat the meat with the spices.

3. Pour in the stock, beef tallow, and water and bring the mixture to a boil. Reduce the heat to low and add the hominy. Cover the pot and simmer for 3 to 4 hours, or until the meat is tender and the flavors have melded together. Skim off any fat that rises to the surface during cooking.

4. Serve the smoked menudo hot, garnished with onion, cilantro, and lime wedges, with the tortillas on the side.

# POZOLE VERDE

Pozole is a Mexican stew traditionally prepared in three different varieties in Mexico: verde, blanco, and rojo. I grew up in a family that ate menudo over pozole, but I've come to love the different kinds of pozole and preparations that accompany each. I started making pozole verde for the family meal in the restaurant with leftover chicken quarters—it was so good, I added it to our seasonal menu. You might not think of pozole as a breakfast dish, but it works well for breakfast or brunch, especially if you've had a few too many cervezas the night before.

2 tablespoons (30 ml) canola oil

1 white onion, diced

3 garlic cloves, minced

2 pounds (908 g) boneless, skinless chicken thighs

1 pound (454 g) tomatillos, husked and halved

2 jalapeño peppers, seeded and chopped

1 bunch fresh cilantro, chopped

1 tablespoon (10 g) kosher salt

1 teaspoon ground black pepper

1 teaspoon dried Mexican oregano

1 teaspoon ground cumin

2 (15-ounce, or 425 g) cans hominy, rinsed and drained

4 cups (960 ml) chicken stock

2 cups (480 ml) water

## FOR GARNISH

Sliced radishes

Shredded iceberg lettuce

Sliced avocado

Lime wedges

1. In a large pot over medium heat, heat the oil. Add the onion and garlic and sauté for a few minutes until translucent.

2. Add the chicken thighs to the pot and cook for about 6 to 8 minutes, turning, until they are browned on all sides.

3. In a blender or food processor, combine the tomatillos, jalapeños, cilantro, salt, pepper, oregano, and cumin. Blend until smooth. Pour the tomatillo mixture into the pot with the chicken and stir to combine.

4. Add the hominy, stock, and water to the pot and bring the mixture to a boil. Reduce the heat to low, cover the pot, and simmer for 45 minutes to 1 hour, or until the chicken is cooked through and tender.

5. Serve the pozole hot with your choice of toppings—my favorites are listed.

# BEEF TALLOW PAPAS CON HUEVOS

Papas con huevos is a dish that's special to me. My mom used to work for my grandfather's tile company, which operated out of my grandparents' home. That meant during summer, my brother and I went to work with her during the week and I got to have breakfast with my Grandpa Hurtado almost every morning. That also meant he was usually cooking papas for breakfast, which was typically served with refried beans and eggs. This version of my grandpa's papas con huevos starts with rendered beef tallow for an earthy, crispy potato that dances around the scrambled eggs and sautéed fresh vegetables. I think my Grandpa Robert would be proud.

½ cup (103 g) beef tallow

2 russet potatoes, cut into ½-inch (1 cm) cubes

1 teaspoon kosher salt

1 teaspoon ground black pepper

1 teaspoon granulated garlic

½ teaspoon smoked paprika

½ teaspoon ground cumin

½ cup (80 g) diced white onion

¼ cup (38 g) diced jalapeño pepper

3 large eggs

½ cup (130 g) Smoky Salsa Roja (page 44)

½ cup (60 g) shredded pepper Jack cheese

¼ cup (4 g) fresh cilantro, chopped

1. Preheat a large skillet over medium-high heat.

2. Pour the beef tallow into the skillet and add the potatoes, salt, pepper, granulated garlic, smoked paprika, and cumin. Stir to incorporate. Cook for 8 to 10 minutes, or until the potatoes begin to soften, stirring occasionally.

3. Stir in the onion and jalapeño. Cook for 5 to 6 minutes, or until the vegetables are soft.

4. In a medium-size bowl, whisk the eggs and salsa roja to blend. Add the eggs to the pan and let them sit for 1 minute. Cut the heat to low and cook the eggs, stirring them every 15 to 20 seconds so they don't stick to the pan. Once they begin to coagulate, stir in the pepper Jack cheese. Remove from the heat and add the cilantro. Serve immediately.

# BRISKET BREAKFAST TORTA

When you think of a Mexican torta on a soft, pillowy telera roll, you probably associate it with milanesa, carne asada, or another hearty meat served atop creamy refried beans, with crema and lettuce. While I love a good torta as much as the next person, I love breakfast even more—and this is the perfect marriage of a Mexican classic with the most important meal of the day.

1 teaspoon kosher salt

1 teaspoon ground black pepper

1 teaspoon granulated garlic

½ teaspoon smoked paprika

½ teaspoon ground cumin

¼ cup (51.5 g) beef tallow

1 Yukon gold potato, cut into
  ½-inch (1 cm) cubes

4 smoked bacon slices

1 telera roll, halved

1 cup (240 ml) canola oil

2 large eggs

½ cup (120 g) Mexican crema

1 tablespoon (1 g) chopped fresh
  cilantro

1 tablespoon (15 ml) fresh lime
  juice

1 cup (256 g) refried beans

8 ounces (225 g) sliced Tex-Mex
  Smoked Brisket (page 89), or
  store-bought, warmed through

½ avocado, peeled and sliced

1. Heat a skillet over medium-high heat.

2. In a small bowl, stir together the salt, pepper, granulated garlic, smoked paprika, and cumin.

3. Pour the beef tallow into the hot skillet and add the potatoes and seasonings. Cook for 8 to 10 minutes, stirring occasionally, until the potatoes are crispy on the outside and tender inside. Test one with a fork to make sure they're cooked through. Remove from the heat.

4. In another skillet or on a griddle over medium-high heat, cook the bacon for 6 to 8 minutes, flipping halfway through. Cook for another 6 to 8 minutes, or until crispy. Remove from the pan, leaving the bacon fat.

5. Toast the telera halves, cut-side down, in the bacon fat for 30 seconds. Set aside.

6. In a sauté pan or skillet over medium heat, heat the canola oil. Crack the eggs into the hot oil and fry for 3 to 4 minutes, carefully splashing oil onto them with a spoon until they are over medium. With a slotted spatula, transfer to a plate.

7. In a blender, combine the crema, cilantro, and lime juice. Pulse 3 or 4 times until well combined.

CONTINUED ➤➤

8. Build the torta by spreading the refried beans on both sides of the roll halves. On the bottom roll, arrange the potatoes over the refried beans. Layer the brisket slices on the potatoes. Place the fried eggs on the brisket and lay the bacon slices on the eggs. Finish with a layer of avocado slices on the top bun and a drizzle of crema across the avocado. Close the sandwich and enjoy the best breakfast torta you've ever eaten.

# PORK BELLY BURNT END CREME BRÛLÉE BISCUIT

The ultimate sweet and savory dessert starts with succulent pork belly burnt ends atop a mountain of brûlée custard, but goes a step further with a flaky homemade biscuit as the foundation for it all. This is a brunch dish I made with my friend Jason from Missouri, who staged (interned) with me for a few months while building his own restaurant near Mizzou. The smoky pork belly bites work really well with the crème brûlée, but you'll want to bring a friend or two to help tackle this plate because it is decadent from the first bite to the last.

### FOR PORK BELLY BURNT ENDS
1 pound (454 g) pork belly, cut into 1¼-inch (3 cm) cubes
1 cup (320 g) honey
1 cup (225 g) packed light brown sugar
6 tablespoons (84 g) unsalted butter, melted
½ cup (120 ml) My Sweet Sauce (page 33)

### FOR CRÈME BRÛLÉE CUSTARD
1 cup (240 ml) heavy whipping cream
3 large egg yolks
¼ cup (50 g) granulated sugar
1 teaspoon Mexican vanilla extract
Coarse sugar, for brûléeing

### FOR HOMEMADE BISCUITS
2 cups (248 g) all-purpose flour, plus more for dusting
1 tablespoon (14 g) baking powder
1 teaspoon kosher salt
8 tablespoons (1 stick, or 112 g) cold unsalted butter, cut into small chunks
¾ cup (180 ml) milk

### FOR GARNISH
Honey
Powdered sugar

1. Preheat a smoker to 275°F (120°C).

2. To prepare the burnt ends, smoke the pork belly on a wire rack for 3½ to 4 hours, or until a dark mahogany color begins to form. Once the pork reaches an internal temperature between 175°F and 180°F (79°C and 82°C), transfer it to a 12 × 10-inch (30 × 25 cm) aluminum foil pan.

3. In a small bowl, stir together the honey, brown sugar, butter, and sweet sauce, then pour the mixture over the burnt ends and toss to coat. Place a lid or aluminum foil on the pan and put it into the smoker for about 2 to 3 hours until the pork reaches an internal temperature between 195°F and 200°F (90.5°C and 93°C) and is soft and pillowy to the touch. Remove from the smoker.

4. To prepare the custard, in a small saucepan over medium heat, heat the heavy cream for 2 to 3 minutes, whisking every 30 seconds to make sure it doesn't scald.

5. In a medium-size bowl, whisk the egg yolks, granulated sugar, and vanilla until smooth.

6. While whisking the eggs constantly to prevent them from curdling, slowly pour the hot cream into the egg yolk mixture. Once combined, pour the mixture back into the saucepan and cook for 3 to 4 minutes over low heat, stirring constantly, until it thickens and coats the back of a spoon. Remove from the heat and let cool, then refrigerate the pan.

**CONTINUED ➤➤**

7. Preheat the oven to 425°F (220°C, or gas mark 7). Line a baking sheet with parchment paper.

8. To prepare the biscuits, in a large bowl, whisk the dry ingredients to combine. Add the cold butter and use a pastry cutter, or your fingers, to cut the butter into the flour until it becomes course and crumbly. Gradually pour in the milk and stir until a dough forms. Be careful not to overmix it.

9. Lightly dust a work surface with flour, place the dough on it, and gently knead the dough for 3 to 4 minutes, folding it into itself. With a rolling pin, roll the dough to a thickness of about ½ inch (1 cm), then use a round biscuit cutter to cut out 4 to 5 biscuits. Place the biscuits on the prepared baking sheet about 2 inches (5 cm) apart. Bake for 12 to 14 minutes, or until golden brown on top. Remove from the oven and let cool for 4 to 5 minutes.

10. To assemble, split a biscuit in half and spoon 2 tablespoons (30 ml) of the custard onto each half.

11. Sprinkle 1 tablespoon (15 g) of the coarse sugar onto each custard-topped biscuit half, then carefully brûlée the sugar with a kitchen torch for 4 to 5 seconds until it caramelizes.

12. Top each half with 1 or 2 pieces of pork belly, drizzle with honey, and dust with powdered sugar.

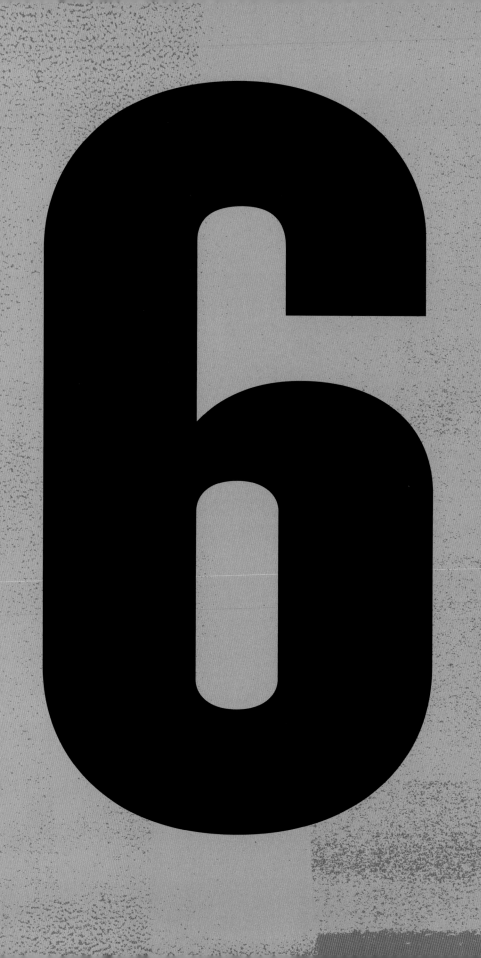

# DESSERTS

# SINCE I FIRST STARTED

cooking in my backyard, I've smoked everything I could get my hands on to test the science behind savory, sweet, spicy, and smoky—including desserts. One of the first things I cooked on a kettle smoker was a lemon blueberry cobbler, and it was an instant hit with friends and family. But not everything works with smoke. In fact, some desserts best complement smoked meats because they have no smoke profile whatsoever. Several of these recipes are instant hits from the restaurant, or seasonal specials that are incredibly easy to make from your own kitchen. From the rich and decadent flavors of Mexican Hot Chocolate Pecan Pie to Orange and Cardamom Biscochitos, there's something here for everyone.

# CHURRO BANANA PUDDING

There are few sweet treats more Tex-Mex, or more traditional barbecue, than this churro banana pudding. The churro "bites" provide little morsels of cinnamon-y crunch between layers of creamy banana pudding custard and fluffy homemade whipped cream. I much prefer using Mexican vanilla extract to generic vanilla extract. Mexican vanilla is two to three times stronger and often offers spicy, woody notes, which complement barbecue incredibly well.

## FOR CHURROS

1 cup (240 ml) water
4 tablespoons (½ stick, or 56 g)
    unsalted butter
½ cup (100 g) granulated sugar,
    plus 1 tablespoon (12.5 g),
    divided
½ teaspoon kosher salt
1 cup (124 g) all-purpose flour
4 cups (960 ml) vegetable oil
1 teaspoon ground cinnamon

## FOR PUDDING

1 (3.4-ounce, or 96 g) box instant
    vanilla pudding mix
2 cups (480 ml) cold milk
1 teaspoon Mexican vanilla
    extract

## FOR WHIPPED CREAM

1 cup (240 ml) heavy whipping
    cream
2 tablespoons (14 g) powdered
    sugar
1 teaspoon ground cinnamon

## FOR SERVING

4 ripe bananas
Caramel sauce or chocolate
    sauce, for serving (optional)

1. Place a wire rack on a sheet pan or line a plate with paper towels. Set aside.

2. Start by preparing and frying the churro bites. In a medium-size saucepan over medium heat, combine the water, butter, ½ cup (100 g) of the granulated sugar, and salt. Bring to a boil, stirring occasionally. Once boiling, remove from the heat and add the flour, stirring quickly until the mixture forms a smooth dough. Transfer the dough to a piping bag fitted with a star tip.

3. In a deep skillet or pot over medium-high heat, heat the vegetable oil to 350°F (177°C).

4. Carefully pipe 2-inch (5 cm) strips of dough into the hot oil, using a pair of kitchen scissors to cut the dough. Be careful not to splash hot oil on yourself! Fry the churro bites until golden brown, about 2 minutes, turning occasionally to ensure they're browned on all sides. Transfer the churro bites to the prepared rack to drain.

5. In a small bowl, combine the cinnamon and remaining 1 tablespoon (12.5 g) granulated sugar. Toss the hot churro bites in the cinnamon sugar until well coated. Set aside to cool, and reserve any remaining cinnamon sugar.

6. To prepare the pudding, in a medium-size bowl, combine the pudding mix, cold milk, and vanilla. Whisk for 2 minutes, or until the pudding thickens. Set aside.

**7.** To prepare the whipped cream, in another medium-size bowl, using a handheld electric mixer, whip the heavy cream on medium speed for 4 to 5 minutes until soft peaks form. Add the powdered sugar and continue to whip until stiff peaks form, about 2 to 3 minutes longer. Do not over-mix. Gently fold the whipped cream into the pudding until well combined.

**8.** Slice the bananas into ¼-inch (0.6 cm) rounds.

**9.** To assemble, layer the bottoms of pint-sized Mason jars with the churro bites and top with banana slices, dividing them evenly. Top with about 3 tablespoons (48 g) of the banana pudding mixture. Repeat the layers until you reach the top of the jars.

**10.** Sprinkle the top of the puddings with any remaining cinnamon sugar, cover, and refrigerate for at least 1 to 2 hours to allow the flavors to meld.

**11.** Serve drizzled with caramel or chocolate sauce, if that's how you roll.

# PORK BELLY CAPIROTADA (MEXICAN BREAD PUDDING)

The history of capirotada in Mexican cooking is murky at best, but it's best known in northern Mexico, where Jewish Mexicans prepared a version during the Inquisition, perhaps as a way to hide unleavened bread. My modern version is similar to traditional bread puddings with one major difference—this one has cheese. I made this for our family meal at the restaurant a few years back and had leftover pork belly burnt ends, which I chopped and mixed into the pudding mixture before baking it, and boy was I glad I did. This recipe works so well with pork, but you don't have to include meat if you want to keep it more traditional. Serve with a scoop of ice cream, if desired.

**8 tablespoons (1 stick, or 112 g) unsalted butter, plus more for the baking dish**

**2 cups (480 ml) water**

**1½ cups (340 g) grated piloncillo (Mexican brown sugar) or (345 g) packed dark brown sugar**

**1 cinnamon stick**

**8 cups bolillo roll cubes (1 inch, or 2.5 cm)**

**2 cups (240 g) chopped Pork Belly Burnt Ends (page 97)**

**1 cup (145 g) mixed nuts (such as almonds, pecans, and walnuts), chopped**

**1 cup (145 g) raisins**

**1 cup (120 g) shredded Monterey Jack cheese**

**1 cup (120 g) shredded cheddar cheese**

1. Preheat the oven to 350°F (180°C, or gas mark 4). Coat a 9 × 13-inch (23 × 33 cm) baking dish with butter.

2. In a saucepan over high heat, bring the water to a boil. Add the piloncillo or brown sugar and cinnamon stick. Cook, stirring, until the piloncillo or brown sugar is dissolved and the mixture is syrupy.

3. In a large saucepan over medium heat, melt the butter. Add the bread cubes and toast until they are lightly golden and crispy. Layer half of the toasted bread cubes in the prepared baking dish. Sprinkle half of the burnt ends, half of the nuts, half of the raisins, half of the Monterey Jack, and half of the cheddar over the bread. Pour half of the piloncillo syrup evenly over the layers. Repeat the layers with the remaining bread cubes, burnt ends, nuts, raisins, cheese, and syrup. Cover the baking dish with aluminum foil and bake for 20 minutes.

4. Remove the foil and bake for 10 minutes longer, or until the cheese is melted and bubbly.

5. Allow the capirotada to cool for a few minutes before serving. Capirotada is traditionally served warm or at room temperature.

# SMOKED BLUEBERRY COBBLER

Blueberry cobbler goes to a new level when cooked in the smoker (stay away from hardwoods like mesquite, though; that can make your cobbler bitter). This is one of the first desserts I ever smoked in my backyard, and it's easy to do in a cast-iron skillet. You can copy this exact recipe and substitute different fruits to have smoked peach cobbler, smoked blackberry cobbler, etc. For an added bonus, serve warm with a scoop of dulce de leche ice cream.

**4 cups (580 g) fresh blueberries**

**1½ cups (300 g) granulated sugar, divided**

**1 tablespoon (15 ml) fresh lemon juice**

**1 cup (124 g) all-purpose flour**

**1 teaspoon baking powder**

**½ teaspoon table salt**

**½ cup (120 ml) whole milk**

**8 tablespoons (1 stick, or 112 g) unsalted butter, melted**

**1 teaspoon Mexican vanilla extract**

1. Preheat a smoker to 250°F (120°C) using a fruit wood or something with a lighter smoke profile, such as pecan or post oak.

2. In a large bowl, combine the blueberries, ½ cup (100 g) of the sugar, and lemon juice. Stir well to mix the blueberries in the sugar mixture. Pour the blueberry mixture into a heat-proof 9 × 13-inch (23 × 33 cm) baking dish or 10-inch (25 cm) cast-iron skillet.

3. In a medium-size bowl, whisk the flour, remaining 1 cup (200 g) sugar, baking powder, and salt to combine.

4. Add the milk, melted butter, and vanilla to the dry ingredients. Stir well until combined. Pour the batter over the blueberry mixture and spread it evenly over the top.

5. Place the cobbler in the smoker and cook for 45 minutes to 1 hour, or until the cobbler is golden brown and the blueberries are bubbling hot. Remove from the smoker and let cool for 10 to 15 minutes before serving.

# ORANGE AND CARDAMOM BISCOCHITOS

Biscochitos are, essentially, shortbread or butter cookies made with lots of sugar, butter, and love. They're the official state cookie of New Mexico, but I grew up eating something similar in north Texas. You can find them at local grocery stores, but they're easy to make and it's even easier to eat an entire batch all by yourself.

8 tablespoons (1 stick, or 112 g) unsalted butter, at room temperature

¼ cup (48 g) vegetable shortening

½ cup (100 g) granulated sugar

1 large egg

¼ cup (60 ml) fresh orange juice

2 tablespoons (12 g) grated orange zest

2 cups (248 g) all-purpose flour, plus more as needed

1 teaspoon ground cardamom

½ teaspoon baking powder

½ teaspoon kosher salt

1 teaspoon cinnamon sugar

1. In a large bowl, using an electric handheld mixer on medium speed, cream together the butter, shortening, and sugar for 2 to 3 minutes until light and fluffy.

2. Add the egg, orange juice, and orange zest and mix well.

3. In a medium-size bowl, whisk the flour, cardamom, baking powder, and salt to combine. Gradually add the dry ingredients to the wet ingredients and mix until a dough ball forms. If the dough is too sticky, add a couple tablespoons of flour. Divide the dough into two portions and shape each into a disk. Wrap the disks in plastic wrap and refrigerate for 1 hour.

4. Preheat the oven to 350°F (180°C, or gas mark 4). Line a baking sheet with parchment paper.

5. Lightly dust a work surface with flour and place one dough disk on it. With a rolling pin, roll the dough to a ¼-inch (0.6 cm) thickness. Use a round cookie cutter (or whatever shape you want) to cut out cookies (you should get between 16 and 20) and transfer them to the prepared baking sheet. Sprinkle with the cinnamon sugar.

6. Bake for 10 to 12 minutes, or until the edges are lightly golden. Remove from the oven and let the cookies cool for 5 to 8 minutes before transferring to a wire rack to finish cooling. Store in an airtight container for up to one week, if you don't eat them all at once.

# OOEY-GOOEY STICKY BUNS

These sticky buns are the definition of decadence. They're everything breakfast is made of, and the perfect dessert to finish off a barbecue meal. While they aren't the ideal "Tex-Mex" sweet finish to dinner, you can spice up the caramel sauce with cayenne or toast the pecans with hot honey syrup for a spicy flair. Sprinkle the buns with additional chopped nuts or drizzle with extra caramel sauce for added decadence.

## FOR BUNS

- 2¼ cups (279 g) all-purpose flour, plus more for dusting
- 2 tablespoons (25 g) granulated sugar
- ½ teaspoon kosher salt
- 1 (¼-ounce, or 7 g) packet instant yeast
- ½ cup (120 ml) warm milk
- ¼ cup (60 ml) warm water
- 4 tablespoons (½ stick, or 56 g) unsalted butter, melted
- 1 teaspoon Mexican vanilla extract
- 4 tablespoons (½ stick, or 56 g) unsalted butter, at room temperature, plus more for greasing the pan
- ½ cup (120 g) packed light brown sugar
- 1 teaspoon ground cinnamon
- ½ cup (55 g) chopped pecans or walnuts (optional)

## FOR STICKY CARAMEL SAUCE

- 8 tablespoons (1 stick, or 112 g) unsalted butter
- 1 cup (225 g) packed light brown sugar
- ¼ cup (60 ml) heavy whipping cream
- ¼ cup (78 g) light corn syrup
- ½ teaspoon Mexican vanilla extract

1. To prepare the buns, in a large bowl, combine the flour, granulated sugar, salt, and instant yeast. In a medium-size bowl, stir together the warm milk, warm water, melted butter, and vanilla. Pour the wet ingredients into the dry ingredients and stir until a soft dough forms.

2. Lightly dust a work surface with flour and turn the dough out onto it. Knead the dough for about 5 minutes until smooth and elastic. Coat a large bowl with butter and place the dough in it. Cover the bowl with a clean kitchen towel and set it in a warm place to rise for about 1 hour, or until doubled in size.

3. To prepare the sticky caramel sauce, while the dough rises, in a small saucepan over medium heat, melt the butter. Stir in the brown sugar, heavy cream, and corn syrup. Cook the mixture for 6 to 7 minutes, stirring constantly, until the sugar is dissolved and the sauce is smooth. Remove from the heat and stir in the vanilla.

4. Coat a 9 × 13-inch (23 × 33 cm) baking dish with butter and pour the sauce into it, spreading it evenly.

5. To finish the buns, once the dough has risen, punch it down and turn it out onto a lightly floured surface. Roll the dough into a 12 × 16-inch (30 × 40.5 cm) rectangle. Spread the room-temperature butter evenly over the dough.

6. In a small bowl, stir together the brown sugar and cinnamon. Sprinkle the cinnamon-sugar evenly over the buttered dough. Sprinkle on the pecans or walnuts (if using).

7. Starting from a long side, tightly roll up the dough into a log. Cut the log into 12 equal-size rolls. Place the rolls, cut-side down, into the prepared baking pan on top of the sticky caramel sauce. Cover the pan with a clean kitchen towel and let the rolls rise for 30 minutes.

8. Preheat the oven to 350°F (180°C, or gas mark 4).

9. Bake the sticky buns for 25 to 30 minutes, or until golden brown and bubbling. Remove the pan from the oven and let cool for a few minutes. Carefully invert the pan onto a serving platter or tray, allowing the sticky caramel sauce to drizzle over the buns. These sticky buns are best served fresh and warm.

10. Store leftovers in an airtight container at room temperature for up to 2 days. To reheat, microwave individual buns for a few seconds or warm in a low oven until heated through.

# LIME ICEBOX PIE

One of my favorite desserts is a lime icebox pie. When I was a kid, we would visit El Fenix restaurant in Dallas, and their most notable dessert was the icebox pie. The lime zest adds a ton of citrus flavor so don't skimp on the fresh ingredients. If you're in a rush, skip the homemade crust and use a frozen crust.

## FOR CRUST

1½ cups (180 g) graham cracker crumbs
8 tablespoons (1 stick, or 112 g) unsalted butter, melted
¼ cup (50 g) granulated sugar

## FOR FILLING

3 large egg yolks
1 (14-ounce, or 395 g) can sweetened condensed milk
½ cup (120 ml) fresh lime juice
1 tablespoon (6 g) grated lime zest
1 cup (240 ml) heavy whipping cream
Lime slices, for garnish (optional)

1. Preheat the oven to 350°F (180°C, or gas mark 4).

2. In a medium-size bowl, combine the graham cracker crumbs, melted butter, and sugar. Stir well until the crumbs are evenly coated. Press the crumb mixture into the bottom and up the sides of a 9-inch (23 cm) pie dish to form the crust.

3. Bake the crust for 8 to 10 minutes, or until lightly golden. Remove from the oven and let cool completely.

4. In a large bowl, whisk the egg yolks until smooth. Add the sweetened condensed milk, lime juice, and lime zest. Stir until well combined.

5. In another large bowl, using a handheld electric mixer, whip the heavy cream on medium speed until stiff peaks form, about 4 minutes. Gently fold the whipped cream into the lime filling until fully incorporated. Pour the filling into the cooled crust and spread it evenly.

6. Refrigerate the pie for at least 4 hours, or until set.

7. Before serving, garnish with lime slices (if using). Slice and serve chilled.

# BANANA PUDDING TACOS

Few things in the culinary world are more Tex-Mex barbecue than these banana pudding tacos. The crunch from a freshly fried flour tortilla, with creamy banana pudding and brûlée sliced bananas on top for even more texture, make this the perfect backyard dessert that's sure to wow your guests. The secret is finding a flour tortilla from a local tortilleria—or making your own—with lots of lard or fat so it fries well. Use a large pot for frying so you can easily make taco shells with a spatula, or bake them in a 350°F (177°C) oven for 8 to 10 minutes for a lighter option.

1 (3.4-ounce, or 96 g) box instant banana pudding mix

2 cups (480 ml) cold milk

1 teaspoon Mexican vanilla extract

1 cup (240 ml) heavy whipping cream

2 tablespoons (14 g) powdered sugar

8 cups (1.9 L) canola oil, for frying

4 (6-inch, or 15 cm) flour tortillas

2 ripe bananas

4 tablespoons (50 g) granulated sugar

1. In a large bowl, combine the pudding mix, cold milk, and vanilla. Whisk for 2 minutes, or until the pudding thickens. Set aside.

2. In another large bowl, using a handheld electric mixer, whip the heavy cream on medium speed for about 5 to 6 until soft peaks form. Add the powdered sugar and continue to whip until stiff peaks form, about 3 to 4 minutes longer. Do not overmix. Gently fold the whipped cream into the pudding until well combined.

3. In a large, deep pot, heat canola oil to 350°F (180°C).

4. Once the oil is hot, one at a time, carefully place each tortilla in the hot oil, pressing down in the middle of the tortilla with a wooden spoon to create a taco shape. Hold the tortilla down for 15 to 20 seconds, or until it holds the shape. Fry for 1 to 2 minutes longer, or until golden brown, then carefully transfer the tortilla to a wire rack to dry.

5. Spoon about ¼ cup (about 60 g) of the pudding mixture into each taco.

6. Slice each banana on a bias into ¼-inch (0.6 cm) slices. Layer half a banana on each taco. Sprinkle 1 tablespoon (13 g) of granulated sugar per taco across the bananas and brûlée them for 2 to 3 seconds with a kitchen torch. Serve immediately.

# MEXICAN HOT CHOCOLATE PECAN PIE

Mexican hot chocolate isn't exactly like the cup of cocoa you're used to around the holidays. It has cinnamon and Mexican vanilla for depth, and a hint of cayenne for a little kick. This recipe takes everything about hot chocolate to another level with fresh pecans and nutmeg. This is one of our most popular desserts at the restaurant and it's simple to make. For even more flavor, pop it in the smoker at 225°F (107°C) for 10 to 15 minutes before putting it into the oven!

1 store-bought piecrust

¾ cup (150 g) granulated sugar

8 tablespoons (1 stick, or 112 g) unsalted butter, melted

¾ cup (233 g) light corn syrup

3 large eggs

2 tablespoons (10 g) unsweetened cocoa powder

1 teaspoon ground cinnamon

½ teaspoon ground nutmeg

¼ teaspoon cayenne pepper (optional)

¼ teaspoon kosher salt

1 teaspoon Mexican vanilla extract

1 cup (100 g) pecan halves

Whipped cream or vanilla ice cream, for serving (optional)

1. Preheat the oven to 350°F (180°C, or gas mark 4).

2. Place the piecrust in a 9-inch (23 cm) pie dish and crimp the edges.

3. In a large bowl, combine the sugar, melted butter, corn syrup, eggs, cocoa powder, cinnamon, nutmeg, cayenne (if using), salt, and vanilla. Whisk until well combined.

4. Spread the pecan halves evenly over the bottom of the piecrust. Pour the filling over the pecans, covering them completely.

5. Bake the pie for 50 to 55 minutes, or until the filling is set and slightly puffed. Remove the pie from the oven and let it cool completely before serving.

6. Serve slices of the pie with whipped cream or vanilla ice cream (if using).

# ACKNOWLEDGMENTS

First and foremost, I am grateful to my Lord and Savior Jesus Christ for leading me down this path in life. I am incredibly blessed to cook for a living and thankful for the opportunity to cook alongside people I love and truly care about.

I am grateful to many people who inspired me and had an impact on the development of this book. Heartfelt thanks to:

All of our team members at Hurtado Barbecue. You are the heartbeat of our company and undoubtedly what makes it special. Recipes are only as good as the people who make them, and the food has always been the second most important ingredient to our success.

Ernest Servantes, my brother-in-barbecue who continues pushing the envelope for me and for other Latinos in the Texas barbecue community. You make me a better cook and pitmaster.

Jim Lero, my first mentor in barbecue, for your continued support, honesty, and shared knowledge of sausage-making.

Tony Aldama, for sticking with me during this crazy barbecue journey and treating my business like your own. You've rolled with the punches and helped us succeed through thick and thin.

Rob Matwick, for believing that a small restaurant can dream big and become the Official Barbecue Restaurant of the Texas Rangers.

Chef Randy White, for your unwavering support over the years, and for always helping me steer the ship without ever asking for anything in return.

Marty Bryan, my friend and mentor, for being an open book and lighting the way for fellow restauranteurs. You are forever changing the dynamic of the food and beverage industry for the better.

Dan Rosenberg, my editor, for helping me understand the need for this book and that I was the right person to write it. This has been an incredible experience, and I am grateful for your guidance and expertise.

Blaine Hurtado, my brother and partner at ANKR Agency. I would not be where I am or who I am without your leadership, brilliant mind, and digital marketing knowledge. I love you, bro.

My mom and dad, Teresa and Gary Hurtado, for always believing in me, even when I didn't believe in myself. And for helping shape who I am as a person, as a father, and as a Christian.

To my wife, Hannah, and my kids, McKinley, Bennett, and Emma, you are my "why." Hannah, we've created something truly special together. I'll never be able to thank you enough for being super mom, my business partner, and my best friend. But I'll spend the rest of my life trying.

# ABOUT THE AUTHOR

**Brandon Hurtado** is a leading authority on Tex-Mex barbecue. As chef/owner of Hurtado Barbecue in Arlington, Texas, he also is one of its most admired hands-on practitioners and passionate ambassadors. His cooking includes recipes with deep roots in the barbecue traditions of Texas and Mexico alongside his own innovative creations that take those traditions in brand-new directions.

Brandon and his wife, Hannah, started serving barbecue in 2018 on the Dallas-Fort Worth pop-up scene, mainly at breweries and microbreweries. They graduated to a food truck in 2019, in downtown Arlington. The food truck was immensely popular, which led in early 2020 to the opening of a brick-and-mortar restaurant, Hurtado Barbecue, in a 120-year-old former railroad station, also in downtown Arlington. Since then the restaurant has been named by Southern Living magazine to its roster of "Top 50 BBQ Joints" across the entire South and by *Texas Monthly* to its list of "Top 50 Texas BBQ Joints," among many other media accolades.

Hurtado Barbecue also is the official barbecue restaurant of baseball's Texas Rangers, with two locations inside the Rangers' Globe Life Field. Brandon has a partnership as well with Taylor Sheridan's 6666 Ranch, and Hurtado Barbecue is the only barbecue restaurant in Texas that serves the ranch's acclaimed beef. In addition, Brandon is the food operator at Sheridan's Bosque Ranch near Weatherford, Texas, where some episodes of *Yellowstone* have been filmed.

Brandon lives with his wife and three children in the Dallas area.

# INDEX